Adventures in Orthodoxy

Dwight Longenecker

Adventures in Orthodoxy

The Marvels of the Christian Creed
and the Audacity of Belief

SOPHIA INSTITUTE PRESS®
Manchester, New Hampshire

Sophia Institute Press®
Box 5284, Manchester, NH 03108
1-800-888-9344
www.sophiainstitute.com

Library of Congress Cataloging-in-Publication Data

Longenecker, Dwight.
    Adventures in orthodoxy : the marvels of the Christian
      Creed and the audacity of belief / Dwight Longenecker.
      p. cm.
    Includes bibliographical references.
    ISBN 1-928832-66-0
    1. Apostles' Creed. I. Title.
    BT993.3.L66 2003
    238'.11 — dc21   2002155836

03 04 05 06 07 08 10 9 8 7 6 5 4 3 2 1

For Don Longenecker

"How good and pleasant it is for
brothers to live together in unity."

Psalm 133:1

Contents

Acknowledgments ix

Introduction: Standing on My Head xi

1. The Man from Missouri 3

2. The Authentic Atheist 13

3. Of Other Worlds 23

4. The Scandal of Particularity 31

5. Arians, Apollinarians, and One-Eyed Pirates 41

6. Purity Is Power 49

7. Agony and Agnosticism 59

8. I Scream, Therefore I Am 65

9. Out of the Frying Pan 73

10. Memes, Magicians, and Manichees 83

11. Up, Up, and Away 91

12. Ambitiously Ambidextrous 99

13. Myths, Movies, and Medieval Cathedrals 105

14. Nature's Bonfire, World's Wildfire 113

15. The Universal Corner Shop 123

16. Encyclopedic Sanctity 133

17. The Metanoia Mentality 139

18. Cannibals, Crocodiles, and Corpses 147

19. Eternity in a Grain of Sand 153

20. Let It Be 159

   Biographical Note: Dwight Longenecker 165

   End Notes 167

Acknowledgments

I wish to thank Michael Craft, Bob Trexler, and Cyprian Blamires for reading this manuscript and offering their excellent comments and criticisms.

I thank Paul Williams, Dom Sebastian Moore, OSB, and John Saward for listening to my ideas and helping me to refine them.

I especially thank Todd Aglialoro and John Barger, first for catching the vision, then editing the book with enthusiasm, intelligence, patience, and hard work. Thanks also go to Stratford Caldecott for putting me in touch with Sophia Institute Press, Joseph Pearce for encouraging the original idea, and Tom Howard for the encouraging words.

I thank Benedict, Madeleine, Theodore, and Elias for helping me to keep my priorities right, and finally I thank my wife, Alison, for her loving support and sense of humor.

Dwight Longenecker
November 1, 2002

Standing on My Head

Picture a fat, middle-aged Englishman trying to stand on his head. This isn't just any Englishman. This is your honest-to-goodness Edwardian Englishman in a tweed suit. With his wide-brimmed hat, drooping moustache, walking stick, and ridiculous pince-nez, he looks like an overblown Teddy Roosevelt. The porcine face puffs as he tries to plant his head on the ground; then the chubby feet, stuck into stout boots, try to kick up into the air. The fat man kicks once or twice, wobbles, then on the third try he's up, feet waving and swaying for balance. His hat is squashed because he forgot to take it off. His tweed cape has fallen over his head. A button on his vest pops off with the exertion; then suddenly the pince-nez fall off, and he instinctively reaches for them, loses his balance, and comes crashing to the ground.

All of this to test the fat man's theory that "any scene, such as a landscape, can sometimes be more clearly and freshly seen if it is seen upside down."[1] The fat Englishman is named G. K. Chesterton, and he wrote those words about a skinny Italian called Francesco Bernardone — otherwise known as Francis of Assisi. Francis was a sort of holy acrobat, a wandering minstrel, a chevalier of the spirit; one of those fools who not only see the world upside down, but turn the world upside down. In his fat English way, Chesterton was a similar sort of clown, and his observation that the world is often more clearly seen upside down is revolutionary.

It's revolutionary, not because Chesterton is a jolly English Che Guevara, but because, when you stand on your head, you revolve and see the world in a different way. Revolutions upset the status quo by challenging the majority view. Any kind of rebellion is both frightening and admirable. Witness our feelings toward the adolescent with purple hair, a surly expression, and a safety pin in his eyebrow. The sort of revolution Chesterton advocates is subversive toward all parties — like a court jester who cracks jokes to those who are solemn and assumes a funereal face for those who are flippant. In fact, the court jester is an excellent example of the sort of revolutionary I'm talking about, because he's an acrobat. He may literally stand on his head and do back flips, but with his jokes and riddles, he also stands on his head symbolically. In so doing, he not only sees things the right way around, but helps others to have a fresh and saner vision of the world, too. Of course, there is a risk in this, for in a world where everyone has gone solemnly insane, the sane person will seem to be a playful idiot, and history shows that society is not kind to such idiots. The prophets, poets, visionaries, jesters, and fools may be laughed at, but they are rarely thanked.

These poetic prophets remind us that for our lives to achieve their full potential, each one of us must go through a revolution. That is, we must learn to see things in a fresh and startling way. Revolutions can be exciting, but they are risky. There is much to gain, but there is also much to lose. Therefore, being cautious as cats, we usually choose to stay right side up and do everything we can to avoid a revolution. We prefer to plod on in our old habits and prejudices, because to launch out into something new is simply too frightening. We are like the seven-year-old who longs to ride the roller coaster but can't get up the nerve.

Sometimes the revolution happens through education. Sometimes it happens through religion. But more often it comes to us as the result of some wonderful or disastrous event in life. We get a promotion, or we get cancer. We hit the jackpot, or we hit rock bottom. We fall in love, or we fall off a ladder. Whether it comes through joy or through sorrow, we have a sudden stupendous vision that turns our world upside down.

Some people pursue this sudden insight and embark on a quest for meaning. They learn to hunger for those daily revelations that amount to daily revolutions. Most of us, however, get a brief glimpse of the Promised Land, then relapse into our usual cautious self, forever wary of that dangerous revolutionary who lurks within and who, for one delicious and dangerous moment, peeped over the parapet.

Revolution is risky, but sometimes resisting it is riskier still. This is true for societies as well as for individuals. The French Revolution reminds us that those aristocrats who refuse to stand on their heads will lose them. We think it would be terrible to change the way we are, until one day the truth dawns that it would be even more terrible if we were to stay just as we are. Suddenly Socrates' words, "The unexamined life is not worth living,"[2] hit us like a punch to the solar plexus, giving us just the jolt we need, first to examine our lives and then to remake them.

Personal revolutions can happen in any area of life. We may suddenly see our job, our marriage, or our waistline in a truthful way for the first time. There are some areas in our lives, however, where it's most difficult to see things in a fresh way. These are the sacred places of our beliefs. Like ancient temples, these sanctuaries are built in stone, and like all holy places, they are inviolable. On their walls are carved the arcane symbols and sacred tenets of the Faith that must never be questioned, even if they're not understood. Religious people acknowledge that they have such sacred spaces in their lives. But nonreligious people have their holy places, too, wherein no blasphemy or heresy is allowed.

Indeed, everyone has some sort of belief system. We all have a pattern in our mind that enables us to make sense of the world. We believe in this pattern because through it we understand everything else. The pattern may be distorted and untrue. It may be conscious or unconscious, but it's there as sure as our heartbeat. Our beliefs may be developed into a complex and beautiful system of religious dogma and devotion, or they may simply be an inchoate set of assumptions we have received from our parents, peers, teachers, and the popular culture. We may not be conscious of our beliefs — indeed we may deny that we have beliefs — but even the denial itself is a kind of belief. Indeed, unconscious beliefs may exert an even stronger hold on us than conscious ones. Thus, we might consciously doubt the infallibility of a pope's declarations, but we would never think to doubt our own.

So all of us have sacred spaces. We all have beliefs, and we instinctively protect and defend those beliefs against every kind of revolutionary threat.

Now, what troubles me about these sacred spaces is that most often they're comfortable. They're furnished with recliner chairs, and the most famous recliner is called the La-Z-Boy. I'm suspicious of any belief system that makes the believer comfortable, because it's probably the construction of a lazy boy. Of course, a comfortable belief may be true, but if you think for a moment, isn't a belief that makes us uncomfortable more likely to be true? An uncomfortable belief is more likely to be true because we wish it weren't true. And if we wish something weren't true, it's less likely that we've made it up.

If we want to find out what is true, we have to get out of the recliner and do some gymnastics. We have to stand on our heads and see the world in a fresh way.

There are two basic belief systems that are comfortable and therefore require a fresh perspective. One belief system says there are no answers, and the other says it has all the answers. The first goes by many names, but it can be called cynical nihilism. Nihilism is the belief that believes nothing, and cynicism is that belief's accompanying emotion. Cynical nihilism holds that there is no real meaning to the universe — or if there is, it can't be known. This bleak belief has been around since the Stoics and is very common. Although it sounds cruel to the point of despair, cynical nihilism is held by a great many people who are otherwise quite cheerful, and this leads me to suspect that cynical nihilism isn't actually a cruel belief, but a comfortable one. And when I stand on my head, I can see this is true, for if there is no real meaning to the universe, there is no real meaning to what I do. I may therefore do whatever I like, and this is a very comfortable belief indeed.

The other and far nobler reason to embrace nihilism is when a person has lived through some unimaginable terror and can't see any meaning within the mindless suffering of millions. It's understandable that the torture and slaughter of the innocents provoke nihilistic rage, but the emotions of rage and ultimate despair assume that there must be some meaning somewhere — even if it seems impossible to discover. Otherwise, why be angry about it? It's true that much suffering seems totally meaningless and void of reason. But this is why such suffering is evil, isn't it? It's evil, not just because people are hurt, but because the evil seems mindless and random. This is a delicate question to try to answer, but perhaps rather than proving that there is no meaning, the existence of evil shows that we think there must be meaning somewhere; and it also shows by contrast how radiant, reasonable, and beautiful real goodness can be.

But most nihilists are not as conscious as that about the emptiness of their belief system. Many people believe there is no ultimate meaning to the universe, but they don't express this belief. Instead they bury their doubt under the many layers of daily life and let their belief be expressed for them. One of their famous archbishops, biologist Richard Dawkins, states the cynical nihilist's creed clearly when he writes, "The universe we observe has precisely the properties we should expect if there is at bottom no design, no purpose, no evil, no good, nothing but pointless indifference."[3]

This sounds grand in a theatrical and tragic sort of way. But have you spotted the joke? If it is true that the universe is random and without purpose, how can Professor Dawkins write books that have structure and purpose? Can the universe really be meaningless? If it were, wouldn't the statement "the universe has no meaning" itself be meaningless? If it's true that there is no meaning, then the whole solemn system that proclaims that there is no meaning is itself nonsense. It's a spectacle of sound and fury, signifying nothing.

If we're locked into the sad belief that the universe is nothing but a random game, to escape this belief we need to stand on our head to catch a glimpse of a universe that is beautiful and open-ended — a universe where a multitude of creative minds are at work and where countless wills either clash or strive to synchronize. This is a universe where anything can happen and life is a constant struggle between mystery and meaning, chaos and design, purpose and free will — a universe where meaning surges forth from every molecule and star. This kind of belief is not taught, but caught. It spreads like laughter at a circus or tears at a tragedy, for it is a trait far closer both to laughter and tears than to rituals and rules. Such belief is not mere mindless adherence to a dull dogma, but the terrible and tender contemplation of an incomprehensible mystery.

That brings me to the second belief system that needs to be seen from a new perspective. If cynical nihilism requires a fresh look, so does formal religion. In the face of cynical nihilism, the religious people come forward wringing their hands. They had always been a bit embarrassed by the seeming irrelevance of their beliefs, and now it seems society has called their bluff. Their response has been to sugar the pill of religion. Religious entrepreneurs have turned the ancient and mysterious Faith into a game show. Their churches are full of people desperate to play *Who Wants to Be a Spiritual Millionaire?*

The more tasteful religious executives have efficiently excised the awkward bits, such as the judgmental God, fantastic miracles, and eternal damnation, and kept the nice bits, such as angels, being good, and making the world a better place.

In doing so, they have watered down the wine and tamed the lion. They have taken a religion worth dying for and made it not worth getting out of bed for.

Still others have retreated from the game shows and tea parties into an underground network of sour, legalistic reactionaries who can do nothing but wag their finger and splutter imprecations against the wicked world. Then they wonder why people don't go to church.

Many people (including many who go to church) view religious belief as impossible, irrelevant, and absurd, but they never stop to consider that it is the impossible which often happens, the irrelevant which turns out to be most necessary, and the absurd which unlocks true meaning. After all, it was one of the world's first theologians who came up with the delightfully anarchic statement, "You ask how I can believe the absurd? Because it is absurd, I believe."[4] No one wants a religion that is easy to believe any more than he wants the ascent of Everest to be accomplished by helicopter. Religion, like mountain climbing, is meant to be difficult.

For religion to have a cutting edge, it has to *glory* in its seeming impossibility, its apparent irrelevance and monstrous absurdity. One mustn't mistake this seeming absurdity for empty meaninglessness. The ancient theologian's absurdity is a riddle with an answer — in contrast to nihilism, which is a riddle whose only answer is that there is no answer.

This is the sort of belief I wish to embrace: a belief that is bracing and revolutionary; a belief that turns our whole world upside down. To encourage this revolutionary way of seeing, this book will reflect on the words of the Christian Creed. This isn't because this is the most respectable way to expose the nakedness of modern thought, but because it's the most embarrassing and ridiculous way. What could be more of a scandal in a mechanical, scientific society than to propose a formula of supernatural dogmas?

In the face of a society that is novel, subjective, and uncertain, I offer the Creed because it is ancient, objective, and sure. The Creed is practical and ordinary, not esoteric and extraordinary. It's both reactionary and revolutionary, out of date and up to date. The Creed is meat and potatoes, not milk and water. It's something you can bite into and debate, something you can love and hate.

Now, my purpose isn't to make you believe the Creed. At least, I don't want you to believe the Creed in that dull way expected by generations of starchy and well-meaning Sunday-school teachers. Their kind of belief in the Creed is like belief in a business contract or a car warranty. Forget it. That kind of dull religion has inoculated millions against the sort of vital belief that revolutionizes the world. They signed up for the Creed thinking it was the end of the story, when it is only the table of contents.

The first job of religion is not to give us all the right answers, but to give us all the right questions. Religion's whole point is constantly to make us stand on our head, to bring us to the brink of that abundant expanse called mystery and allow us to teeter there on the edge of the darkness. The point of all the rigmarole is to take us beyond the exercise and into the unexpected. If the seemingly dull Creed upsets the nihilist, it also turns all forms of pedestrian orthodoxy upside-down, because it bursts with magnificent meaning, unexpected and eternal insights. Like a concise cathedral crammed with hidden nooks and corners harboring endless nuances of light and shadow, the Creed teases with everlasting antinomies and paradoxical possibilities.

Those who reject dogma see the Creed as a narrow constitution that chokes truth. Instead it is the elegant expression of truths that have been discovered through conflict. Many suspect the Creed because they think it constricts the exploration of truth. I see the Creed as the starting point for that exploration. The Creed is not the end of the journey; it is the map for the journey. It is not a final definition of belief, but a springboard from which to discover the ancient, ever-youthful truth. The Creed provides a fixed point, a starting block to run the race. It is not a chair, but a ladder; it is not a mattress, but a trampoline.

Contemplating the Creed turns the whole world upside down. This concentrated confession is like a laser of light to a confused mind. It makes us squint. Then if we dare to open our eyes, its tiny beam reveals everything in a new light. If the Creed is doing its work properly, it will wake us up. Like one of those churchwarden's wands with a feather on one end and a knob on the other, it will either tickle us awake or give us a knock on the head.

Adventures in Orthodoxy

*People have fallen into a foolish habit of
speaking of orthodoxy as something heavy,
humdrum, and safe. There never was anything
so perilous or so exciting as orthodoxy.*

G. K. Chesterton

I believe in God, the Father Almighty,
Creator of Heaven and earth,
of all things seen and unseen,
and in Jesus Christ, his only Son, our Lord,
who was conceived by the Holy Spirit,
born of the Virgin Mary,
suffered under Pontius Pilate,
was crucified, died, and was buried.
He descended into hell,
and on the third day rose again.
He ascended into Heaven
and is seated at the right hand of God,
the Father Almighty.
He will come again to judge
the living and the dead.
I believe in the Holy Spirit,
the holy Catholic Church,
the Communion of Saints
the forgiveness of sins,
the resurrection of the body,
and life everlasting.
Amen.

Chapter One

The Man from Missouri

I believe . . .

I've never been to Missouri. Yet wherever I turn, I find myself living there. Missouri, as any home-grown American will tell you, is the "Show Me" state: because the Man from Missouri won't believe it unless he sees it. Missouri Man is the archetypal squinting, chin-rubbing yokel who won't be taken in by nobody, no way, nohow. If Missouri is a flat state in the middle of America, it's also a flat state of mind in the middle of our culture.

Sadly, Missouri Man is not only a local yokel; he's everywhere now. He can be found at every level of society from the street cleaner to the sophisticate. He personifies a cynical and suspicious attitude that has found its way into our society, one that irritates, not like a pebble in a shoe, but like a hole in a shoe. It irritates as an absence, not as a presence. As a result of this empty space, no one is to be trusted. No one has the answers. Nothing can be believed.

Now, there's nothing wrong with healthy skepticism. Healthy skepticism is honest and robust. It unmasks the charlatan, defrocks the fraud, suspects the superstitious, and hoots at the hypocrite.

Healthy skepticism takes potshots at all forms of pomposity and pretense. Have you noticed how children are healthily skeptical? When they watch the mayor strut by in his cockaded hat or the bishop glide in looking like an upholstery exhibit, they may be amused, but they're not impressed. A child is skeptical because he is curious, and he is curious because, at heart, he is a believer. In his discovery of the world, the child believes truth is possible to discover, and so he healthily sniffs out anything that masks or distorts the truth.

But a cheerful suspicion of humbug isn't the same as sour skepticism. Unhealthy skepticism doesn't actually believe there is such a thing as truth. There are some skeptics who explicitly deny that there's such a thing as truth, but have you noticed how the same belief exists in more fuzzy forms? You needn't be an austere anarchist to disbelieve in the possibility of truth. It's enough, like the urbane theologian, to smile through the sherry and say, "What works for you is true for you." What this theologian is suggesting is that all truths are of the same value, but isn't this another way of saying that truth is of no value? For how can all things be equally true? Can blue be orange depending on your point of view? Can a dose of arsenic "work for me" and "not work for you"? Can two plus two equal seven if you simply alter your perspective? Can philosophy be reduced to a shrug of the shoulders and, "You say tomAYto and I say tomAHto"?

The conviction that there's no final truth takes other fuzzy forms. Some deny the possibility of truth by asserting that what is true is the same as what is attractive. Truth is attractive, but the advertising industry and a pretty face teach us that what is attractive isn't always true. All that glitters is not gold.

You can also deny that there's such a thing as truth by observing that truth changes from one age or culture to another. Certainly the expression and emphasis of truth takes different forms at different times and in different cultures, but that doesn't mean the truth changes. An American may call it turquoise; an Englishman may call it aquamarine. They may argue whether they are referring to a color or a gemstone, but to both, bluish green is still bluish green.

Part of the problem is that the Man from Missouri suffers from a "merely mechanical mentality." For him facts are the only truth, and the only certain thing is that which can be explained. By explaining how a mysterious thing works, the Man from Missouri believes he has explained the mystery away. But there's a problem with this, isn't there? Have you ever noticed how the more we probe into a mystery, the more mysterious it becomes? It seems that every answer only produces another question. Whenever we discover how something in the natural world works, there's always another factor left to explore. Doesn't this lead to the conclusion that things are more than what they're made of, more than the way they work? The very act of trying to explain the mechanics of a mystery only pushes us further into the unknown, and if it pushes us further into the unknown, it hasn't solved the mystery, but has compounded it.

One has to admire the tenacity of the Man from Missouri. When faced with a mystery that made our ancestors wonder and worship, the Man from Missouri (whether he's a sophisticated scientist or a cynical sophomore) pushes back his ball cap, scratches his head, and says, "Shucks, there must be some other explanation" — and proceeds to poke and prod and cook up another theory. This laudable tenacity mustn't be sniffed at, but what is lacking in our hero's approach is any sense of belief — that instinctual awareness or lurking suspicion that there might be more to life than flywheels and cogs and chemical reactions. That anyone can have such a mechanistic way of seeing the world is itself a mystery, and it forces us to ask where such a prosaic mind set came from.

It's easy to blame that hard-bitten old dame Science, who has taught us that we should only trust what we discover ourselves. It is true that science can be cynical, but true science is open, inquisitive, and unafraid of the unexplainable. No, science is not the problem; and it's often part of the solution. Professor Dawkins is right when he says good science is both poetic and passionate for truth.

We may study the development and the decay of philosophy or pin the blame on sociology, psychology, Marxism or capitalism or Darwinism or any other "-ology" or "-ism," but our pin will have missed the point. Unbelief may have used all the "-isms" and "-ologies," but the disease of unbelief is deeper and older than all of them. Unbelief is not particularly modern. There have always been human beings who have found it impossible to believe. Perhaps the ancestry of Missouri Man can even be traced back to the beginning of mankind's struggle. If so, then Missouri Man is as ancient as Cro-Magnon Man.

Ever since Cain, we have found it difficult to believe. The reason has nothing to do with science. Quite simply, it's difficult to believe because it's difficult to obey. Belief is never simply an intellectual exercise. As rational beings, we know that to acknowledge something as true means that it must change our life. If something is true — really, utterly, and radiantly true — it demands our total allegiance. If something is eternally and magnificently true, it was here before I was and it must change me; I can't change it. No matter who the person is, or in what age he has lived, belief that demands obedience is, and always will be, a terrifying and exhilarating prospect.

Even the mere word *obedience* is a shock to the heart. It's enough to make you throw a book across the room. The word makes us think of pursed-lipped old nuns ready to thrash timid children into submission. We see hordes of jackbooted thugs goose-stepping to the commands of their demonic overlords. We imagine gullible religious devotees submitting to bizarre beliefs. We think of the young automatons of religious sects and the quivering woman shielding her children from the demands of an outrageous husband.

These are examples, not of obedience, but of domination and subservience. The obedience that goes with belief is something different. It's an inquisitive, open-ended, and youthful virtue. The word *obedience* comes from the Latin *obedire*, which means "listen to." True obedience is a kind of curiosity. It's a fresh alertness, a childlike eagerness to listen and learn. It's the voice of deep calling to deep. It is a human heart open to the drawing and calling of a timeless and universal power that the ancients could only call Love.

To say "I believe" is more than belonging to a suburban special-interest group that raises funds for charity. To believe is more than forcing ourselves to suspend our incredulity long enough to accept a few archaic metaphysical propositions. It's more than signing on with a spiritual Santa who offers goodies rather than demanding goodness. In the most ancient Creed, we say with magnificent simplicity, "I believe in God, the Father Almighty, maker of Heaven and earth, of all that is seen and unseen."

Now stand that sentence on its head. Take the last part first. Make the ending your beginning, and you have a simple phrase: "I believe in all that is seen and unseen."

This is the first step: to develop a state of mind that is open to all things. A mind that accepts rather than rejects; that sees possibilities, not problems; a state of mind that is instinctively inquisitive, not cynical, and sees meaning rather than absurdity. The first step is not to believe all the specifics, but simply to Believe. To Be. To Live. To Be Alive. To Believe.

To believe in all things seen and unseen is to accept all that is real, both in the natural and in the supernatural realms. It means embracing every morsel of matter, from each grain of sand to each gargantuan star. It means being full of wonder at all things invisible — from atoms and angels to molecules and miracles. To believe in all things seen and unseen means accepting that the visible and invisible realms are intermingled in a marvelous and mysterious way. It means gasping with delight at the wonderful and frightening realization that all things are possible. This is the innocent, unembarrassed, and blessed state of the believer: His heart is open to everything on earth and in Heaven, and he plunges in to be overwhelmed by it all, crying, "I believe!"

The romantic pastor Schleiermacher put it in terms philosophical. To believe is "to accept everything individual as a part of the whole and everything limited as a representation of the infinite."[5] Dostoevsky's tender monk Alyosha knew what it meant to believe in all things seen and unseen. After the death of his friend Zossima, he stumbled outside and was touched by the interconnection of earth and heaven.

> The vault of heaven, full of soft shining stars, stretched vast and fathomless above him. . . . The gorgeous autumn flowers, in the beds around the house were slumbering till morning. The silence of earth seemed to melt into the silence of the heavens. The mystery of earth was one with the mystery of the stars. Alyosha stood, gazed, and suddenly threw himself down on the earth. He did not know why he

embraced it. He could not have told why he longed so irresistibly to kiss it, to kiss it all. But he kissed it weeping, sobbing and watering it with his tears and vowed passionately to love it, to love it forever and ever. . . . But with every instant he felt clearly, as it were tangibly, that something firm and unshakable as that vault of heaven had entered into his soul.[6]

How can the bland despair of the Man from Missouri compare to such passion? How can the everlasting boredom of the nihilist compare to such a vibrant life? How can the yawn-inducing rituals of staid religiosity compare to this heart-rending vision of reality? In response to "I believe in all things seen and unseen," the Man from Missouri can only shrug his shoulders and say, "I believe in nothing I can't see." And this is only a short hop from the nihilist, who says, "I believe in nothing." As a result, both the nihilist and the Man from Missouri have nothing, and may ultimately become nothing.

The timid religionist will also run from this vision of reality to take refuge in his ecclesiastical kennel. He does so because this kind of belief is bigger than all religion and dogma and so threatens those secure boundaries. Oblivious to their fears, the believer cries with open arms, "I believe in all things seen and unseen!" and in saying so, like Alyosha, he possesses all things and will one day become one with that One by whom all things exist.

Still we draw back, afraid at what we might lose, but never seeing what we may gain. We're more frightened of the glory we don't know than of the misery we know. Belief stands and beckons like a magnificent cherubim, but still the Man from Missouri whispers in our mind that we might be fooled. We might be taken in.

There is certainly proper cause for caution, but there's also cause for levity, because gullibility is even more widespread among those who aren't religious. Witness how nonbelievers fall for the smooth promises of politicians, marketing men, astrologers, and self-help gurus. Compared with these medicine men, the sensible priest with his dogma, liturgy, and canon law looks downright prosaic. The true believer is not gullible. He is healthily skeptical of charlatans, frauds, mind games, and tricks — especially the mind games and tricks he is likely to play on himself.

The believer runs the risk of being gulled, but even if we are fooled and taken in, is there anything so very terrible in that? If it's all a huge cosmic joke, isn't it better to share in a joke than not to laugh, or never to have heard the joke at all? If belief is an absurd mistake and there is not a Judgment Day, then nothing has been lost; but if there is a Judgment Day, it will be far better to have believed too much than not to have believed enough. Even in this life, which is better — believing in all things seen and unseen or believing in nothing? In what will you live and move — all things radiant in earth and heaven or absolute zero? Will you believe and choose delight or not believe and choose despair?

Of course, to believe in all things seen and unseen requires a risk. The Man from Missouri is a belt-and-braces man. He carries double insurance, locks the door at night, and never takes a risk. The true believer, on the other hand, is forever taking risks. He knows that change is the only sign of being alive. He takes the leap of faith. He jumps from the trapeze stand into the void, believing that his partner's arms are there.

Still the voice of fear whispers in our hearts, warning that such extravagant belief will demand something from us. We might be led down a trail that demands "not less than everything." We may have to face even death itself. (Of course that's a reason to embrace belief as much as it is an excuse to avoid it. We're going to face death either way.) In any case, no one is pretending that sacrifice isn't part of the bargain. There's no small print in the Creed. The One who calls makes it clear that your fears are justified. Indeed, everything will be required. Not one shred of doubt, cynicism, unbelief, or fear may remain. Not a scrap of false pride, bigotry, narrow-mindedness, jealousy, or rage will be allowed to stay. Not one morsel of squalid lust, envy, or bitter resentment will be permitted to rot and fester in your heart. All of it must go, and it will not go without a kind of burning torment. It's true that the way of belief requires both ecstasy and agony. Joy can never be real without sorrow, and new life is available only to those who are willing to die.

And so I believe. With defiance and fear, like the primitive tribesman who stares at the stars and trembles, I believe. I believe because through belief I can say yes to all things, and "yes is a pleasant country."[7] "I believe because all that is seen and unseen" sings out that there is someone other than myself in the universe. I believe because the yearnings in my heart and the spiritual instincts of all humanity reach out for that Someone; and I believe because belief is the only courageous way of life that will help me to discover who that Someone is and how I can come to know him.

Chapter Two

The Authentic Atheist

. . . in God, the Father Almighty . . .

I have a curious respect for the outspoken atheist. He wears his denial of God on his sleeve with a certain panache. He defies the deity as Cyrano de Bergerac duels with death. The atheist courageously contradicts the instincts of the entire human race in order to declare the nonexistence of God. Like a latter-day Don Quixote, the atheist rides off to joust with the windmills of superstition, religion, and the fairytale deity. With touching absurdity, the crusading atheist overlooks the fact that he spends time and effort refuting something he doesn't believe exists. That's why I like atheists. The rebel in me admires someone who paddles upstream, and when he attempts to scale a waterfall in his canoe, my admiration for him only increases. The campaigning atheist is like that. Despite all the evidence, despite the universal religious instinct of the human race, he acts on his solemn belief that there's nothing solemnly to believe in. But that's also why I don't believe he's really an atheist: he believes too much and cares too much for truth.

Is there such a thing as an utterly authentic atheist? I think so. I have a dreadful feeling that there exists a secret subspecies of human beings who have lost their spiritual capacity completely. These authentic atheists don't profess belief in God, but neither do they profess disbelief in God. Instead they seem unaware of the concept altogether. They don't hate the Church or say the Bible is a fairytale. They don't spit out bigoted remarks that blame the Pope for the Holocaust or missionaries for murder. They don't demolish arguments for the existence of God, say the universe is random, or accuse Billy Graham of being a simpleton. They don't attack religion; they seem simply unaware that religion exists.

These are the authentic atheists. They plod through life, eating, working, shopping, breeding, and sleeping, and God never seems to flit across their consciousness. Members of this subspecies may be sparkling sophisticates or ill-bred boors. They may be the decent and moral folks next door, or they could be despicable murderers. In a frightful way, it doesn't matter. If they exist, perhaps they have bred and spread like alien body-snatchers and exist in our midst like spiritual zombies — indistinguishable in the teeming mass of humanity except to those few who see them and tremble.

Then there are the secret atheists. These are the ones who have adopted the best and most sinister disguise of them all: they have become religious. They lurk in the stalls of cathedral choirs as well as in the stalls of the Christmas bazaar. These religious atheists sing and speak the words of religion, but don't believe in a God who is real in any sense of the term. They worship instead a deity of their own imagining — a comfortable grandfather in the sky, or a Great Being who gives them pleasant dreams, but makes no demands. The God of earthquake, wind, and fire — as well as the God of the still, small voice[8] — is an alien and unreal creature to these soulless devotees of a soothing religion.

I'm spinning stories and jesting to make a point. Of course all humans have souls, even if they neglect them. But if my hunch is right that some people never give God a thought, we are witnessing a radical and tragic decline in the human race, for it is subhuman to exist without a god of some kind. Religion is a universal part of the human condition. In every culture and language — from primitive tribesmen who grunt at the stars to sophisticated technicians who grunt at computer screens — the religious instinct persists in a most stubborn way.

When you look at the human religious instinct, doesn't it seem quirky and unexpected? If we're only brutes, why do we all possess this tender and mysterious instinct to fall on our faces before our Maker? If we're animals, why do we see spiritual beings everywhere? Dogs sniff and lift their legs at trees; men see mournful dryads imprisoned there. The real religious instinct in man is a kind of madness and is as beautiful and bizarre as those other forms of human madness called music, poetry, laughter, and dancing.

What is this surprising inclination to worship and sing to some Almighty Being? What instinct causes men to build a temple, Stonehenge, or Chartres, a basilica or a Baptist chapel, a ziggurat, the Parthenon, or Angkor Wat? There's no human society anywhere in time or place where religion is nonexistent. In fact, you could almost use the instinct and ability to pray as the mark of what it is to be human. Perhaps we should be called *homo orans* instead of *homo sapiens*. When a humanist declares his independence from religion, he isn't exalting his humanity; instead he's declaring himself subhuman, for the whole of human history and culture declares that a glorious and eccentric part of being human is to be religious.

The Man from Missouri reduces the wild and wonderful phenomenon of religion to the idea that God is merely the projection of humanity's need for the ultimate sugar daddy. His theory goes like this: Primitive man needed to magnify ordinary authority figures such as fathers and kings by projecting them into Heaven to create an almighty being to comfort him in the face of the everlasting darkness and reward him with eternal life. In other words, the whole religious phenomenon is a huge case of corporate wishful thinking.

There are three problems with this theory. First, it's incredibly dull. The Man from Missouri is not the sort of person you want to go on holiday with.

The second problem is that this doesn't describe the god of most religions. In most religions, the gods are not sugar daddies. They don't reward their children with pink clouds of cotton candy in the afterlife. Instead they are cruel and violent supernatural beings who are more likely to devour you than to delight you. Even the Christian God, who purports to be a loving Father, threatens final judgment and eternal damnation. This isn't what I would have invented if I were thinking wishfully. Given that the god of most religions is a lion, not a pussycat, perhaps it's the atheist who is engaged in wishful thinking.

There is another problem with this line of thought, and it's the most disturbing. Saying that God is the result of a corporate wish is a kind of bathtub-drain mentality. Everything, bubbles and scummy bath water alike, can go swirling down into it until nothing is left. The problem can be stated like this: If God is simply a case of wishful thinking, then everything we consider good, beautiful, and true might also be explained by the same devilish logic. Indeed, everything bad, ugly, and false can be magically whisked away.

So, for instance, if God is the result of our wishful thinking, morality is merely the expression of our need to control our society; patriotism, a projection of bigotry and xenophobia. Beauty is no more than my own erotic urgings projected outward, and truth itself is simply my sad attempt to impose order and meaning on the chaotic and meaningless cosmos. If all is wishful thinking, this strange phenomenon we call love is little more than a projection of our own pitiful, infantile needs. Perhaps even the physical world is real only within my own perception. We know the senses can be reduced to electrical impulses to the brain. The whole beautiful, cruel, tender, hilarious world could be nothing but a fizzle in my head.

Perhaps the idea that God is a projection of the human imagination is a reversal of the truth. The alleged atheist has strayed into a hall of mirrors and gotten lost. He's mistaken a reflection for reality. It might look as if God is a projection of our imagination, but the truth is that we are a projection of his imagination. The ancient texts confront and correct this very problem. They warn us against making God in our own image and specifically tell us that we are made in his image. It's an easy mistake to make, for either position looks as if it might be true, but then reflections do look like the real thing.

Whether you think God is a projection of man or man a projection of God depends on where you start. If you start with yourself, God is a projection, but if you start with God, you are the projection. This being the case, you must ask yourself which is the more logical starting point — you or God? Who is more likely to have been there first?

Arguing for the existence of God has always been a yawn. The most the philosophers can do is infer that God exists. But who wants to dance with an inference? Can you rebel against a logical proof? Why debate the existence of light when such things as eyesight and color exist? Besides, if one has developed a believing mentality, the first step of saying not only "I believe" but also "I believe in God" may not be so difficult.

When philosophers and New Age gurus speak of God, they use majestic and enigmatic terms such as "Ultimate Being" or "Eternal Essence." The problem with God's being an "Ultimate Other" or a "Force of Dynamism" is that we can't imagine such a thing. It's our nature to imagine the unimaginable using images, and when we start to imagine the "Elemental Essence" or the "Spirit of Cosmic Being," we end up getting a mental picture of a huge spray of cheap perfume, or a vast tapioca pudding in the sky. An impersonal force seems like a sensible starting point, but most people find swimming in cosmic ectoplasm rather sticky.

Nevertheless, modern sophisticates tell us that as primitive people grew wiser, they come to see that God is really an impersonal force. But doesn't the reverse seem more likely? Isn't it more sensible to assume that the grunting humans emerging from the ooze were the first to sense that God was also a kind of ooze? Wouldn't the first religious instinct be a dim awareness that there was some sort of "impersonal force" behind all things? It was later, as man developed into a cultured, colorful, storytelling creature that he figured out that the Force has a Face.

This is how infants develop. First there is the big, fuzzy, loud thing with a red spot in the middle, and then as the child grows, he learns to recognize his father's face, complete with beard and bulbous nose. Isn't this the way with all things and all ideas? They develop from simple to complex and decay from complex to simple. If this is so, then the simpler idea that God is an impersonal force must be the more primitive. Certainly it's possible to move from belief in a personal God to belief in an impersonal force (many intellectual clergymen take this step), but such a move is always a decline, not a development. It is a slip backward, not a step forward.

While images for God are necessary, it's also true that all our images of God are ultimately inadequate. They don't go far enough, because God is beyond our images and our imagining. The most profound words spoken about God are the ones that remind us that we can't speak about God. As soon as we say, "God is this," we must also say, "God is not this."

But while this is true, it's also true that we can say certain things about God. We can discuss what we don't know, and we can discuss what we're discovering, and we can discuss what we hope to discover. Sometimes our language is vague and hypothetical. At other times our language is precise and theological. Then at times our language about God is poetic storytelling. With all these ways of talking about God, we're using both complicated and simple images of the truth to make sense of what is mysterious, immense, and awesome. The best images for God are the simplest and the oldest, because these are the least likely to be taken literally. If we call God "Father" for instance, we know immediately that the image isn't good enough, because we think of our own hopeless, funny, and pathetic earthly fathers.

The simplest and oldest images for God are also the best because they're the most universal and basic. A baby delighting in his father's face is the simplest and most beautiful reason for calling God "the Father Almighty." The Father is the first "other" person most of us get to know. (It takes a long time for a child to figure out that he and his mother are actually two different people!) Therefore, what could be more simple and ingenious than to call the Ultimate Other Being "Father"? Jesus and the Jews say this image was revealed by God himself. The Jews thought God was like a father, but Jesus reveals that God actually *is* the Father, because he calls Jesus "my beloved Son,"[9] and Jesus quite naturally calls him "Papa."[10] In this way, Jesus not only taught us to call God "Our Father," but he showed us that at the very core of God's identity is fatherhood.

Feminists and anthropologists from Missouri give a more expedient explanation. They theorize that, like all other simple people, the old men of a patriarchal culture cast God in their own image. The Jews were bearded mini-monarchs who sat around on cushions, being waited on, so they perceived God as a bearded grandfather of them all, sitting on clouds, being waited on.

This is a reasonable theory, and the history of religion shows that humans have a real tendency to create gods in their own image. But what if this reasonable theory is also just a mirror reflection of reality? Instead of God the Father's being a reflection of our fathers, what if our fathers are reflections of God the Father? What if our own existence which came about from our father making love to our mother rests on the fact that the whole cosmos has an ever-loving Father? What if the Big Bang was a masculine explosion of delight, love, and creative force on a cosmic scale, implanting a seed of life into all things? If so, God really is the Father of all, and that minute and precious element we call "life" is a tiny droplet of God implanted by divine power into each and every cell of creation. If this is so, then calling God "the Father Almighty" isn't just an outmoded metaphor; it's the very essence of his divine identity, an expression of his connection with all things living, and an indispensable description of who he was and is and ever shall be.

Nevertheless the intelligentsia object to God's being called "Father." Could it be that, like all adolescents, they're going through a rebellious stage? Are they simply like the teenage girl who's embarrassed when her father dances at a wedding? Do these father-phobes stomp their feet and slam their bedroom door, or do they just write a book about the evils of patriarchy?

At the bottom of this entertaining dispute is the real objection to God's being called "Father": to suggest that God really is, in some sense, our Father, is to say, not only that he's a personal God, but that he's in a personal relationship with all those whom he calls his children.

Suddenly the question of God's being personal or impersonal isn't an academic debating point; it's an explosive question of the heart. For if God is "the Father Almighty," I'm faced with Someone who can't be ignored. An eternal force is easy enough to ignore. A cosmic pudding is abstract and safe. But if the Force has a Face, then that Face may be looking at me, and if he's looking at me, it's very possible he's looking *for* me. Therefore, when I say, "I believe in God, the Father Almighty," I'm not simply stating a truth about God; I'm taking a part and stepping on stage in the midst of a drama of immense importance.

If God really is "Father," then I'm in a relationship with him, whether I like it or not. As Martin Buber has observed, I'm in a relationship with an intimate other being, and that relationship makes me who I am.[11] That relationship may be one of rebellion and rage, or it may be one of reconciliation and return. If I'm rebelling against the Father, I may express the rebellion in furious rage. I may choose to ignore him. Or, like the son in the famous story, I may simply choose to run away from that compelling paternal presence. In doing so, I join that dignified band of fugitives called the human race. To run away is perhaps the most honest and wholesome thing to do, and it isn't wasted, for as all the great stories tell us — from *The Wizard of Oz* to the Prodigal Son — sometimes we must run away before we can really turn toward home.

Chapter Three

Of Other Worlds

. . . Creator of Heaven and earth . . .

In *The Universe in a Nutshell*, Professor Stephen Hawking tells us that alternative worlds are a real possibility.[12] Fans of fantasy, re-joice! Children of Narnia, come out from hiding! Science-fiction geeks and hobbit-lovers, step out of your paperback world with pride. Walking through wardrobes, falling down rabbit holes, and traveling to other worlds is possible after all! The news is out: Mod-ern physics has joined forces with ancient metaphysics; science has caught up with science fiction.

I realize Professor Hawking would probably not be as unre-served in his enthusiasm for Narnia, Wonderland, and Middle Earth as I am. When we affirm that God is the "Creator of Heaven and earth," Missouri Man will blame us for believing in fairytales, for naively holding to a three-tiered universe with Heaven in the sky, earth in the middle, and Hell underground.

But did anyone ever believe our world is really like that, or were they just telling stories? When ancient people said they be-lieved in Heaven and Hell, did they really think Hell was under-ground and Heaven could be located on the other side of the clouds? I doubt it. I doubt that ancient people who dug mines were surprised when they didn't find fiends roasting sinners in lakes of fire underground. In my experience, most religious people cope with metaphors fairly adeptly. It was the poor literal-minded cosmonaut who seemed surprised when he went into outer space and didn't see angels and God sitting on a throne.

When a person says he believes in Heaven and earth, he means that he believes in a material realm and a spiritual realm. He proposes the existence of a spiritual realm, not because he wants to live in fantasy land, but because a spiritual realm is necessary to account for his experience. In other words, his decision to accept the spiritual realm is essentially scientific, not religious. The hypothesis fits the evidence. The idea of a spiritual realm provides possible explanations for all the weird and wonderful experiences that human beings keep reporting and which *Fortean Times* — that chronicle of the unexpected — so delightfully records.[13]

When faced with fish falling from the sky, crop circles, visits from aliens and angels, ghosts, fairies, monsters, miracles, and apparitions, the Man from Missouri says such things either have "natural" explanations or they are all in the mind. But those who believe in the heavenly or spiritual realm are simply saying that there are more realities than can be perceived with the human senses. This is common sense for any boy who has ever had a nightmare or blown a whistle that only his dog could hear.

One who believes only in the visible leaves no space for the invisible realm, but if you believe in all things seen and unseen, you can allow for both types of reality and also allow for strange interactions between the two. If you believe a spiritual realm exists, you needn't be surprised at monsters or mystical experiences. You make room for devils and demons as well as for grace and goodness. Has someone seen a statue weep or bleed? Has a saintly girl's body not decomposed even after a hundred years, and does it still smell like posies when it should smell like putrefaction? Perhaps. Has someone been healed by the power of prayer? Have millions seen angels, watched the sun spin, or seen a thousand-year-old prophecy fulfilled? Could be.

This isn't to say that you have to take all these things at face value. The believer doesn't immediately and unquestioningly accept every unusual happening as supernatural. Like any sensible person, he knows "visions" are more likely if a person is insane, tired, or drunk. The true believer is fully aware of how easily people are duped and deluded. When faced with an extraordinary occurrence, the ordinary believer looks for every natural explanation first. However, because the believer allows for "all things unseen," he has possible explanations for the unexplainable.

Furthermore, the person who believes in "all things seen and unseen" has an added and interesting dimension to his life. Believing in the spiritual dimension is like putting on a pair of 3-D glasses. Things jump out at you. Hidden possibilities emerge. Everything surges with an inner meaning and secret life. The difference between the cynic and the believer in this respect is that the cynic sees *through* everything, while the believer sees *into* everything. So, for example, when the cynic sees bread and wine, he sees only crushed wheat and crushed grapes, while the believer sees the crushed body of his martyred Master.

The Man from Missouri may accuse the believer of being superstitious. He could be right. It's possible to be superstitious, but which is worse: to be superstitious or to be cynical? A superstitious person rarely does anyone any harm, whereas a cynical person poisons everyone he meets. There's a charming hopefulness about superstitious people. Can you actually dislike a person who kisses the bones of a saint or spends a lifetime waiting to photograph the

Loch Ness monster? However, while there are some superstitious believers, there are many more who are properly skeptical of the supernatural, but not so dogmatic as to rule it out altogether. In fact, the vast majority of the human race believe in ghosts, but don't believe their eyes when they see one. This isn't superstition, but common sense. It's simply allowing, like Hamlet, who saw a ghost, that there are more things in Heaven and earth than Horatio's philosophy had dreamt of.

That there is a spiritual and a physical dimension brings a personal God back into the conversation. "Creator of Heaven and earth" echoes the first verse of the Hebrew creation story, which says that God is the Maker of both Heaven and earth. In other words, he made both the spiritual and the physical realms. The fundamentalists tell us with great solemnity that God made the heavens and the earth in one week, beginning on Sunday, October 23, 4004 B.C. The evolutionist tells us with an equally awed whisper that the world evolved over an unimaginably long period. Although the fundamentalist and the evolutionist would hate to be lumped together, their mind set is the same, because they both have to explain everything with dates and charts and time periods. The evolutionist mesmerizes us with large amounts of time, while the fundamentalist is equally amazed by the youth of our earth.

These stand back-to-back like two madmen strapped together and unaware of the other's existence. In this matter, isn't it safer simply to stand apart from them both? Why should we accept their self-confident statements when common sense tells us that no one can be sure exactly how or when the world was created, because no one was there when it happened?

They say that the opera isn't over until the fat lady sings. When it comes to creation, it isn't over until the fat man sings, and I can think of two fat men who might sing a duet. The first fat man is G. K. Chesterton, who describes his discovery of a Creator thus:

> I had always believed the world involved magic: now I thought that perhaps it involved a magician. And this pointed to a profound emotion always present and subconscious; that this world of ours has some purpose; and if there is a purpose, there is a person. I had always felt life first as a story: and if there is a story there is a storyteller.[14]

The other fat man is the great philosopher Thomas Aquinas. He sings in subtle harmony, *"Quidquid fit, causam habet"*: "Whatever happens has a cause."[15] If you go back far enough in time, there must come a time when there's no time. There comes a Cause that had no cause. When we say in the Creed that God is the Maker of Heaven and earth, we are simply stating the monumental fact that God is the Great Monumental Fact. He's the First Cause, the One before whom there is no other. That he made Heaven and earth is what we believe. That is the poetic fact. How he did it is where the prosaic fiction comes in.

It's entertaining to guess how he made the heavens and the earth, and down through the ages, mankind has been engaged in all kinds of storytelling to do just that. It may well be that he spoke creation into existence in one week, long, long ago, and after each day's work said, "That's good!" Or perhaps he sang Heaven and earth into creation as Aslan did Narnia.[16] Perhaps he planned all things with the exquisite precision of an engineer, or perhaps like some marvelous Michelangelo, he is passionately and obsessively at work on a million projects at once. Then there is the dull creation myth that says the world simply evolved into what it now is over a very long passage of time.

Adventures in Orthodoxy

I'm content that God may have ordained some sort of evolutionary process to bring his creation to full flower, but what I can't believe is that the whole thing happened as a matter of chance. I know many people believe this miraculous story without the slightest doubt or hesitation. They accept the infallible authority of their biology teachers without demur.

Now, I admit to being a believer even to the point of gullibility and superstition at times, but I simply don't have that much faith. I've tried to believe the Gospel according to Darwin, but I can't.

With not one nudge or hint of a wink that the theory is a huge practical joke, I'm supposed to believe the solemn story that the whole of creation, with its vast intricacy, evolved over billions of years simply by random chance? It looks leaky. It seems to me the theory has been pieced together with a bit of bone here and a shard of fossil there and held together by the glue of ingenuity and the artificial awesomeness of great amounts of time. In this, I confess, I'm an incurable doubter and cynic. I'm in favor of leaps of faith, but I'm not that athletic.

The problem with random evolution is that it requires faith in random meaninglessness — and this from the people who blame religious folks for having "blind" faith! Do people really believe that even one simple organism can develop from a mindless sludge of mud by chance, given enough time? If one simple organism cannot develop by chance from the primordial soup, how much less can a complex organism, or the whole delicately balanced, interrelated, vastly complex, and beautiful natural world? Doesn't everyday experience tell us that on their own, complex things don't come from mud — they return to mud? Doesn't common sense tell us that complexity disintegrates into simplicity and simplicity, on its own and by random, never develops into complexity? Where is the boy who noticed the emperor was naked?

When I affirm that God is the maker of Heaven and earth, I repudiate the idea that the whole of creation came about by chance. Happily, the Creed leaves it there. As a believer, I don't have to take it further than this, and as such the believer's Creed is far more flexible and open-minded than the materialist's. The believer can have God and nature, but the materialist must only have nature. The believer's system, like his mind, is therefore open, while the materialist's is closed.

That God is the Creator tells me not only what God did, but who he is. When I say I believe in the "Creator of Heaven and earth," I've discovered another image of the personal God. At the heart of his being, he is a maker, a progenitor, and an artist. He's a fat opera singer, a lusty painter, and a tender violinist. He's an athlete, an intellectual, a poet, a gardener, and a storyteller. Above all, in all, and through all, he's creative and creatively alive. He's constantly making all things new, yet he has never spoken the same word of creation twice. Perhaps across the realms of time and space, throughout the universe, new worlds are springing into being. Maybe the whole fantastic work of creation is burgeoning here, there, and everywhere with a prodigious, wasteful, bohemian sort of artistry. God isn't a static, once-and-done creator. He's a constant, creative, dynamic source, ever ancient and ever new.[17]

Furthermore, he's a junkman, a refuse collector, a salvage expert, a recycler, and a thrift-store manager. Not only is he making all things fresh and new, but he's forever busy reclaiming and remaking all that was lost and broken. He delights in turning trash into a treasure. He collects the cast-offs, recycles the wrecks, and redeems the ruined, clapped-out remnants of creation. He's economical and wasteful at the same time — spending an enormous amount to recover one pearl, one treasure lost in a field, one wedding ring, or one child lost in the crowded and wicked world.

If he's the maker of Heaven and earth, he's also the maker of me, for I'm a part of Heaven and earth. Indeed, I'm one of those hybrid marvels called humans, in which Heaven and earth are jumbled together in a heady and maddening mixture. He has made me from dust, but breathed into me the breath of life. I believe in the Maker of Heaven and earth because I see Heaven and earth in conflict, not only all around me, but also within me. I'm aware that the blend of brute beast and everlasting beauty clashes within me.

This war between Heaven and earth is constant and severe. The clash in me has broken my heart. I'm one of the walking wounded. I leak. But if God is not only the artist, but also the salvage expert, there's hope he might rescue and restore me. Therefore, although I lie in the gutter, I may look up to contemplate the stars. Although I'm a creature of earth, I'm also a child of Heaven; and the Hound of that Heaven may one day find me and lead me on the long journey home.[18]

Chapter Four

The Scandal of Particularity

. . . and in Jesus Christ, his only Son, our Lord . . .

One autumn afternoon, I went for a walk with a Buddhist monk.
This young man from Australia had all the cool reserve and lofty
detachment that I expected in a Buddhist monk. We discussed
monasticism and meditation and found much in common. Then
we began to discuss what we actually believed.

The Buddhist had been cool. Suddenly he became cold.

He had been happy to discuss his karma, but not to explain his
dogma. When the conversation turned to the topic of God, I tip-
toed up to the idea of a personal God. The Buddhist understood
the proposition, but didn't think it a probability. When I told him
that Christians actually believe the transcendent God took particular human form in a unique way at a particular place and time,
the Buddhist drifted into a polite silence. I was embarrassed. I felt
as if I had exposed my gullibility, committed an error in taste, or
maybe even blasphemed.

The intelligent Buddhist is sensible to shy away from the idea
that the personal God took human form in Jesus Christ. Buddhists
aren't the only ones. Indeed there are plenty of Christians who

also shy away from this most robust and embarrassing of doctrines. I respect their honesty. In fact, I'm a bit suspicious of the smiling, squeaky-clean Christians who seem to have no problems with the incredible idea that God became a particular person in Palestine two thousand years ago. I worry because, if they don't have a problem, I wonder whether they have ever really thought it through. When it comes to the idea of the Incarnation, honest believers can have honest doubts.

The intellectually outrageous idea that God jumped on the roller coaster of the human race is called "the scandal of particularity." With this term the theologians admit that it's an intellectual embarrassment to suppose that a transcendent God would step into human history around 7 B.C. and be born of a peasant girl in a smelly stable in a backwater of the Roman Empire. I take their point. Like the sheep in the stable, I feel sheepish when I view the Christ Child. I find myself a bit envious of the Buddhist, whose religion isn't encumbered with something as embarrassing as an Incarnation.

But what's embarrassing is often true. That's why it's embarrassing. What embarrasses us also kicks us awake. When the parish priest turns out to have a fondness for Elvis Presley impersonation, we're surprised, delighted, dismayed, and curious to know more. But if we know anything about the priest, it suddenly fits. The truth clicks into place. So that's why he dyes his hair black and takes so many holidays in Nashville!

There's something wild and unpredictable about truth. When everything is cut and dried, don't you suspect that you're being offered something attractive, but artificial? Buddhism, for example, is a most attractive religion. It's exactly the sort of religion one would make up if one had to devise a religion. It makes sense. It's cautious. It's controlled, rational, and pure. It has a beautiful,

spiritual teacher who gave up his kingdom for truth. It has a sublime spiritual method, a refined morality, and an elevated explanation for the origin of pain. It offers a sad but realistic-sounding
solution for suffering and gives a sensible explanation for what
happens after death.

Real Christianity, on the other hand, is none of that. It's particular and unpredictable, contradictory and messy. It stands the
predictable religions on their heads. This is the maddening and
delightful thing about Christianity; but because it's upsetting and
awkward, it's real. That's why Christianity feels truer than Buddhism, because it's more like life itself.

If truth is always stranger than we expect, it's also more ordinary than we expect. Once we've seen that something is true (no
matter how strange it seemed at first), it becomes as ordinary and
real as baked beans or bicycles. It belongs. It fits. If it's a central
truth, it not only fits, but everything fits around it. A central truth
not only makes sense, but it makes sense of everything else. So, for
instance, if you didn't know better, your everyday experience of
life would lead you to conclude that the world was flat. The sun
clearly moves in an arc over an earth that looks flat. But then one
day someone tells you that the world is not flat, but round. You
might find this difficult to believe, since it contradicts what your
everyday experience has led you to expect, but when you take the
leap of faith and accept that the world is spherical and not flat,
everything else suddenly makes more sense, too. "So that's why
those who sail around the world wind up where they started!"

A similar thing happens when we contemplate the idea that
the eternal God could become one particular person in human
history. Our whole instinct leads us to deny such a preposterous
proposition. But why should the idea that a universal becomes
particular necessarily be so difficult? How could the universal be

33

real if it did not become particular? As the old washerwoman replied when she was asked what she was thinking, "How do I know what I'm thinking unless I says it?" It's the nature of everything unspoken, vague, invisible, and universal to be particularized. In fact, when you see it this way, isn't it more of a scandal if the universal does not become particular?

All around us we see the miracle of the universal becoming particular, over and over again. So, for example, the universal principles of music become particular when Charlotte sits down to play Chopin. At that point we don't think it scandalous that the great universal "Music" has become limited to a particular combination of keys on a particular keyboard played by a particular set of ten fingers and heard by a particular set of ears. Indeed, if music were not particularized in this way, we would never know music at all. Furthermore, to be real, the music has to be made particular over and over again. The miracle of the universal music becoming a Chopin étude, a jazz riff, or a Broadway tune is always and everywhere the miracle of the universal becoming uniquely particular.

But we are talking about God, not Gershwin, and the main reason we perceive a problem with God's becoming particular is that he is supposed to be "up there" while we are "down here." This way of looking at Heaven and earth isn't big enough. It isn't small enough either. Blake saw the world in a grain of sand and Heaven in a wildflower.[19] He held Heaven in the palm of his hand and eternity in an hour. For him the universal was particular all over the place, and that was the definition of its being universal. The visible and the invisible are not separated into "up there" and "down here." The universal and the particular are intermingled all the time and in every place, from the vast reaches of outer space to the microscopic reaches of every cell.

Doesn't all the evidence point to this conclusion? All of creation has its predictable visible element tumbled together with a surprising invisible element. In physics, Bell's Theorem assures us that there are connections inside reality that can't be explained by the normal categories of touch, contact, and contiguity. Things affect each other in ways that go beyond the usual categories of physical causality. As soon as the scientists explain one part of the physical realm, some vast or minute mystery opens up, and an unexpected inconsistency makes them think again.

If the visible and invisible are co-mingled in this mysterious way, why should we suppose that God is totally separate from the physical world he created? This isn't to say that the created world is God, nor that it contains God, or that God depends on the world he created. This is just to say that God isn't separate from the physical realm. While he's outside it, he's also inside it. He's both the force that made it and the force that holds it together.

If God exists with, and in, and through the physical realm, why is it so difficult to believe that he might emerge from that realm and take a particular physical form at a particular place and time? It's only a more specific focus of the kind of presence he has always maintained in the world. We imagine the Incarnation as Jesus coming down from Heaven to this world like an alien or an angel. It seems more probable to me that he was here all along, and that he simply decided to step out from where he was hiding so we could see him.

This "putting on" of human flesh seems astounding to us, because we imagine that God, like the jazz singer sings, "ain't got no body." In other words, that he is so nonphysical that he in fact regards the physical world as distasteful and dirty. We imagine that becoming incarnate is, for God, a strange and disagreeable activity — that to do so, he might have to wrinkle his nose and put on rubber gloves. But what if the truth is exactly the other way around? Maybe God enjoys becoming incarnate. Maybe part of God's personal nature is a curious delight in dressing up. Maybe he puts on human flesh with the same seriousness and whimsy as an actor puts on his broad hat, hose, and rubber nose to play Cyrano de Bergerac and save the wounded world. Maybe in countless worlds throughout the universe, God is putting on the garment of flesh in a multitude of forms we can never imagine. Maybe he prepares each world for his Incarnation in gradual, creative ways, as he did in our world through the rough-and-tumble family history of the Hebrews.

Some religious historians like to point out that the myth of the incarnate God was commonplace among ancient peoples. Practically every religion had stories of incarnate gods and goddesses. Some actually had myths about gods who took human form, then died and rose again to save the world. The early Christians simply adopted the prevailing religious language and mythology, say the comparative religionists.

But similarity doesn't demand connection or causality. I'm not descended from or related to all other myopic, bald-headed men with large noses. The similarities within religions don't disprove the Christian story. If anything, it's just the reverse. The fact that the Christian story echoes the earlier stories suggests that the older, more tentative stories were simply a rehearsal for the real thing. They were hints and guesses at the riddle, and Christ was the final answer.

Therefore, similarity between the Christian story and other incarnation tales isn't surprising or incredible. What would be surprising and incredible would be for the Christian story not to have any shared characteristics with other world religions. The fact that it does validates its authenticity and universality.

The Scandal of Particularity

Still we're told that the Incarnation can't be a historical fact. It's simply a religious myth like all the others. The problem with that theory is that the story of Jesus Christ doesn't read like a religious myth. Unlike the great religious myths, the Gospel story is rooted in ordinary people and real places. Even if it could be shown that the Gospel writers got some of the details wrong, the whole point was that they bothered with the details at all. Some people say the Devil is in the details; for the Gospel writers, the Divine was in the details. Their intent (and the point of the whole New Testament) was to show that God had taken flesh as a particular historical person, a Jewish rabbi from Nazareth called Jesus. If only the Gospel writers hadn't told us about particular Roman rulers and particular towns in Judea, we could sigh with relief and write the whole thing off as yet another beautiful religious myth.

The scandal of this particularity is shocking because of the humility it implies. How could God, who is above all and isn't dependent on any created thing, come into the world and be dependent on a Jewish peasant girl for his every need? "Did God cry for breast milk, then burp, smile, and gurgle?" asks the Man from Missouri. The Christian shrugs his shoulders, gives an embarrassed grin, and says, "That's where the logic leads."

We struggle with such a concept because we think such condescension contradicts God's essential nature. But what if it were the other way around? What if this act of humility confirms God's essential nature? What if this act, above all others, reveals exactly what God is like? What if those countless Madonnas holding a Christ Child for us to view are the clearest picture we'll ever get of God himself? Wouldn't that be a crazy and wonderful surprise after all those tiresome thunder gods and devouring earth mothers — all those Obi Wan Kenobi Forces-That-Are-With-You[20] or the distant deities of the East?

To turn things on their head, it's that hiccupping Infant who shows us what real power is like. While he's independent of his creation, this God chose to burst that truth from the inside out, limit himself by place and time, and put himself at the mercy of his creatures. We said he was the ultimate Father. Here he's the ultimate Child. The Man from Missouri dislikes paradox, but a paradox always slaps us awake with a new perception of truth. Saying, "We believe in Jesus Christ, his only Son, our Lord" means that while God remains the Master, he takes the form of a slave. The Almighty becomes all meek. Furthermore, it is by giving up his sovereign power that he actually confirms his power most powerfully. Anyone can hold on to power using force. Only the Omnipotent can prove his total power by giving up power totally — and yet his will is still accomplished.

This is the mark of the truly great, that everywhere it becomes small. We call this virtue humility, and we're surprised that God is humble. To be humble isn't to be a groveling peasant or a sniveling simpleton. Humility is the radiant quality of being totally and utterly oneself — in other words, it isn't being a simpleton, but being simple.

God must be simple. In other words, he must be completely one and completely himself without any duplicity or complication. If he is himself, he is humble, and the logical action of his humility is for him to take the lowest possible form while still retaining his essential image. If this is the case, then for God to take particular human form isn't an extraordinary act of charity on the part of an essentially aristocratic deity; it's the characteristic act of a humble deity. In other words, for God to become a human being actually fulfills one dimension of who God is. In that sense, what we call the miracle of the Incarnation is as natural and pure as water flowing downhill.

The Scandal of Particularity

This scandalous doctrine, therefore, confirms God's character — it doesn't contradict it. The fact that we call Jesus Christ
"God's Son" is the historical reality that confirms and consolidates
God's reputation. It's his calling card, his résumé, his *pièce de
résistance*. This reversal of our preconceptions stands the whole
world upside down. If God became man in a village of Palestine
two thousand years ago, then the whole way I look at myself and
my world is changed. Suddenly the heart of religion isn't about
formulas and forms, rituals, rules, and regulations. It's about becoming real — as real and as particular as God became. Suddenly
religion isn't about dull conformity, but radical nonconformity. It
isn't about fitting in, but about sticking out; for if everyone else, by
his total egotism, is seeking to be a little god, then to be a little
person is to be a nonconformist. Perhaps this is what the Man-
God meant when he said we had to become like little children to
enter his kingdom.[21]

So if I want to be like God (which, if humans are made in
God's image, is simply to be truly human), I'll look for the path of
simplicity. I'll find ways to be totally and honestly myself. Furthermore, I'll seek out those who are also simple and simply themselves. I'll find ways to serve without counting the cost and seek
sacrifice without reward. This is why the saints show us what God
is like, while sinners only show us what *they* are like. The saint is
someone who has discovered the secret of becoming like God. He
has learned to lower himself in imitation of the Incarnation.

Saying, "I believe in Jesus Christ, his only Son, our Lord" isn't
the dull recitation of an outmoded dogma. It's a dramatic means of
plunging headfirst into this scandalous and beautiful belief. It
means getting my hands dirty and becoming more particular and
more real than I ever imagined. It means becoming all that I was
meant to be.

Do you want to be real? Then contemplate the Incarnation, for the mystery of the Incarnation proclaims the beautiful truth that reality is below you and within you, not above you and beyond you. Do you want to find God? Then contemplate the Incarnation, for the Incarnation is the living proof of that universal principle that you must go down to meet God, for God always comes to us from below, and we must stoop to find him.

Chapter Five

Arians, Apollinarians, and One-Eyed Pirates

. . . who was conceived by the Holy Spirit . . .

When the Pope visited Athens and was met with religious riots in the streets, he was taking part in a venerable Greek religious tradition. The Greeks have been rioting over religion for centuries. It's a wonderful and eccentric part of their culture. It may seem odd to us that the Greeks take to the streets over arcane matters such as the primacy of the Bishop of Rome or the double procession of the Holy Spirit; but the Greeks probably think it odd that the English take to the streets in the passionate defense of foxes, or that Americans take to the streets with marching bands and majorettes to honor the homecoming queen.

Compared with the icy disdain most Anglo-Saxons nurture toward any form of religious enthusiasm, the Greek passion for a theological riot seems as gutsy and wholesome as their taste for goat cheese and olives washed down with ouzo, or their habit of breaking crockery at weddings. Down through the ages, the Greeks have rioted over religious truth because they believed religious truth was not only possible, but also important. In the third and fourth centuries, the early Christians, like all brothers and sisters, fought bitterly. Like siblings quarreling over a will, they fought over their theological inheritance, and the result of the battle would determine what kind of world their children would inherit.

The debates centered on just what exactly the birth, life, and death of Jesus Christ really meant. It wasn't a matter of theological nit-picking. The Greeks — natural philosophers that they are — understood that the answers affected everything. The debates were conducted by colorful characters: patriarchs, politicians, emperors, and archbishops. The quarrels were complicated by philosophy and theology, politics and power, but beneath the fascinating complications, there were really only two sides to the debate, and these two sides reflect the two sides of virtually every philosophical debate.

These two sides are illustrated in the famous painting by Raphael called *The School of Athens*. In the center of the painting stand the philosophers Aristotle and Plato. Aristotle points down to the earth, and Plato points up to the heavens. Aristotle thought earthly realities more real than heavenly realities, while Plato thought the heavenly realities more real than the earthly.

When the early Christians asked who Jesus really was, they were given the answer by Jesus' immediate followers that he was God in human flesh. But when they got the simple answer that Jesus was God incarnate, they wanted to define just how Jesus was God incarnate, and that's why they started fighting. Was Jesus a man who seemed godlike, or a god who seemed manlike? Was he a very good man, but not fully God, as Arius claimed, or was Apollinarius right that Jesus was fully God but not fully human?

On one side, the Arians, like Aristotle, pointed to the earth. On the other side, the Apollinarians, like Plato, pointed to Heaven.

The clash between the two points of view seemed irreconcilable, but in any irreconcilable quarrel, the way through is for both sides to admit they're wrong, and then for both sides to admit that they're right. In other words, both sides were partially right and partially wrong. To find the full truth, they had to see both sides and embrace both truths simultaneously — even if doing so seemed contradictory or paradoxical. The truth is always stereoscopic. Error, on the other hand, has single vision. That's why pirates always wear eye patches.

In the debates about who exactly Jesus Christ was, the ones who were piratical were heretical. They were one-eyed. They could only see one truth and not the other. The Arians denied that Jesus was truly God. The Apollinarians affirmed that he was truly God, but denied that he was truly man. Both sides refused to lift their eye patches to see the truth in its radiant, three-dimensional splendor.

This ancient debate matters because these two opposing points of view stand as symbols for almost every category of debate. So in our distorted age, the greedy materialist believes only in the physical realm, while the gullible spiritualist believes only in the heavenly realm. All these errors, whether ancient or modern, spiritualist or scientist, evidence the difficulty in reconciling the spiritual realm and the material realm. This clash between the two is the very stuff of religion, and any religion that avoids the conflict misses the whole point.

Neither is the conflict confined to the realm of philosophy and theology. I face the conflict between earth and Heaven with the realization that religion is about both God in Heaven and the idiot next door. Religion involves my prayer book and my bankbook, my sex life as well as my prayer life. The conflict is there, because in me and in everyone else, there is a creature of earth and air struggling for flesh and spirit to be reconciled.

The Greeks rioted in the streets because they realized how important it is to resolve the clash between Heaven and earth. When

I was younger, I was taught that the whole world hung on the principles of physics. Now I believe the whole world hangs on the principles of metaphysics. If the spiritualists are right, this world doesn't matter, but if the materialists are right, nothing but this world matters. Ironically the results of both views are the same: for if this world doesn't matter, I can do what I like, but if there is nothing but this world, I may also do what I like, for there is (literally) no Hell to pay. In other words, if I see like a pirate, I may end up behaving like a pirate.

This clash between Heaven and earth is solved by the conception of a Child who was both fully God and fully human. Jesus Christ is the physical solution to a metaphysical problem. In biology, conception means a fusion of the characteristics of two individuals into one, and in Christian theology it means the fusion of two worlds into one. At the core of this concept is the belief that at a particular place and time, Heaven and earth were merged. The universal and immortal became particular and mortal; outer space entered inner space, the timeless entered time; and that which is spiritual and divine penetrated that which is physical and human. The old categories of eternal and temporal, spiritual and physical, heavenly and earthly were abolished. Christians believe that God hovered over a young woman and conceived a new being — a fusion of Heaven and earth — the one called both Son of Man and Son of God. As the ancients observed, in Jesus Christ we have not merely a good man, but the God-Man.

As a result, a new relationship between earth and Heaven exists. The old dualities are irrelevant. A new world order is possible.

Because of the ultimate implications of this astounding insight, it was vitally important to get the details of this dogma right. That's why the stubborn bishop Athanasius in the fourth century insisted on the problematic and paradoxical formula that Jesus

Christ was fully God and fully man. A compromise would have been far simpler. A different definition could have made peace, but any other form of words wouldn't have expressed what the first Christians truly believed had happened.

Jesus himself had said that he came to bring not peace, but a sword.[22] The fusion of God and man in Jesus Christ reconciled Heaven and earth, but it also divided humanity into those who accepted this reconciliation and those who refused it. The early Christians understood that only a fully stereoscopic vision of Jesus as the God-Man would unite the opposing factions and change the world forever. If Jesus Christ was only a good man, then the world hasn't changed. If he was God who only seemed to be a man, then, again, the world hasn't changed. But if Jesus Christ is truly God and truly man, then a bit of Heaven has been planted in earth and the clash between Heaven and earth is over forever. Suddenly Plato and Aristotle could stop quarreling and embrace one another. The chasm was bridged, the wound healed, the war over.

This is why Christianity, in its full-blooded, rumbustious dogma, is subversive and revolutionary — not because it preached freedom for slaves or because the martyrs refused to swear allegiance to the Emperor; not because beautiful virgins and venerable old men went to heroic deaths or because Jesus taught people to be meek and mild. All these things had happened before and elsewhere. Christianity was revolutionary because it taught that in Jesus Christ there was a stunning new relationship between all things seen and unseen.

This is why Christianity is unique among world religions. Every other religion tries to bridge the gap between earth and Heaven through some technique. Some call for their devotees to make bloody sacrifices to please the gods. Others call for the flesh to be subdued by obedience to a strict code of laws. Others call for their followers to forget the suffering of the flesh in order to achieve a higher consciousness. In each case, they try to bridge the gap between flesh and spirit; but in Christianity the gap is bridged for us. It's accomplished at the moment the Holy Spirit conceives the God-Man.

This reconciliation also explains the curious contradictory nature of Christianity. Christians have always insisted that both the flesh and the spirit are good. Christian monks may purify the flesh through fasting, but they also pamper the flesh with feasting. The Church teaches the virtue of celibacy, then turns around and praises marriage, making love, and making babies. She makes religious laws, then says it isn't laws but love that matters. Christians are happy to kiss both the tattered robe of St. Francis and the embroidered cope of the bishop. They kneel both in the hovel where Christ was born and in the cathedral where he is adored. Christians are taught to love their bodies and to laugh at their bodies. In other words, they are trained to keep their eyes firmly on Heaven and their feet firmly on earth. Through the reconciliation of Heaven and earth, Christians constantly realize that the spiritual and the physical are intertwined. The heavenly gentleman and the earthly lady are forever spinning in a complex and beautiful dance.

Because of this interplay between the physical and the spiritual, the Christian way seems like walking a tightrope between the excesses of the flesh and the excesses of the spirit. This isn't the case. The Christian way is more like the trapeze than the tightrope. We're not called to tread a delicate balance between the spiritual and the physical, but to leap off the platform and fly through the air, borne up by the strong arms of both. This is more difficult and more dangerous than walking a tightrope. But if it's more difficult and dangerous, it's also more exhilarating and beautiful.

The conception that fused earth and Heaven was accomplished by the power of God that Christians call the Holy Spirit: that fiery, chthonic force that rumbles at the heart of creation from the dawn of time. The first words of the book of Genesis hint that the same brooding, gestating, and conceiving power was there at the beginning. The Holy Spirit constantly broods over the bent world to bring forth new life. Those who wanted a force have got one. The Holy Spirit is "the force that through the green fuse drives the flower."[23] He is "the dearest freshness deep down things."[24] He's there pressing like an impatient lover to infuse every life and enthuse the whole world.

That same creative force broods over the chaotic darkness of my life, not forever and for no reason, but right now and for a clear reason. And if it has a reason, it has a will; and if it has a will, it has a personality; and if it has personality, it must be a person. As the Holy Spirit Person conceived a fusion of earth and Heaven in the God-Man, so he writhes and wrestles to reconcile earth and Heaven in me. My duty and my destiny are to wrestle with him and, as when Jacob wrestled with the angel, to rise from the struggle battered, but blessed.[25]

Chapter Six

Purity Is Power

. . . born of the Virgin Mary . . .

Last year I visited the National Gallery of Art in Washington, D.C.
I decided to start off exploring the modern collection. Red leath-
erette drainpipes were stuck on the wall, a plastic box held fruit
pies made out of plaster, enormous mobiles hung from the ceiling,
and the floor was littered with carved shapes — as if some gigantic
baby had left his blocks lying around. The walls displayed huge
canvases: all wonderfully colorful, anarchic, and meaningless.

I found the whole thing rather tame. I was surprised not to find
three tons of carved animal fat, a pile of trash, or a squashed hat.
Where was the dog-doo collection? Where was the slattern's un-
made bed? Why couldn't I see a desiccated sheep in a tank of form-
aldehyde, a two-headed monkey, or Jack the Ripper's undershirt?
Isn't an authentic modern-art gallery supposed to be a cross between a peep show, a freak show, and an insane asylum? In that
sense, the modern wing of the Washington gallery was a letdown.

The security guard was a young black guy with a suspicious eye
and a smart grin. I asked him which gallery he liked best. He said
he preferred the early Italian stuff. So I asked whether he had a

favorite painting. He smiled and suggested I find the *Small Cowper Madonna*. I took his suggestion and made my way to a room half full of paintings by Raphael. There in one corner hung an exquisite painting of the Madonna and Child. Raphael is famous for his Madonnas, but this one was smaller than most. It was more intimate and the beauty more immanent. The setting conveyed all the natural innocence and simplicity of a woman with her child; but somehow this one was different. Mary's enigmatic expression and the luminosity of the colors hinted at the extraordinary mystery that was locked within that most ordinary scene.

I was captivated. For a moment time was transposed into eternity, and in that mixture of pigment and paint, the mysterious theory that God at one point took human flesh became almost tangible.

It made me wonder later why we consider anything to be beautiful at all. Why should we look at a landscape, a painting, or another human being and feel that surge of delight, wonder, and desire which we call "beauty"? Modern aesthetic theory follows the old wives and says, "Beauty is in the eye of the beholder." But what if it's the other way around, and beauty is actually in the thing we're beholding? Isn't that what our experience tells us? We see a sunset, a Raphael Madonna, or a beauty queen, and we gasp and say, "That's beautiful!" We don't say, "As I regard that object, my cultural and educational background has conditioned me to interpret my inner feelings as something called beauty."

Beauty isn't in the eye of the beholder, but in the essence of the beautiful object. That's why we all feel that beauty takes us outside ourselves and puts us into contact with something greater, more mysterious, and more wonderful than we thought existed before.

In a way, that picture also says something about every painting and poem and piece of music that aspires to be beautiful. The object of art particularizes beauty. It makes beauty real and physical. That Raphael painting was full of grace and truth, and I beheld its glory; and that's what Christians say about the relationship between Jesus and God. He is God's work of art. He incarnates beauty and truth. In him the source of beauty, truth, and glory comes alive.

As I gazed on that luminous Madonna, I made contact not only with something beautiful, but with Beauty. It was also an astoundingly intimate experience of purity and power. For a moment I glimpsed a kind of purity that was both as soft as moonlight and as hard as diamonds. I suddenly realized that purity, like all things beautiful and refined, is an acquired taste. Like the fragile beauty of a Mozart aria, or the calm, exquisite beauty of a Chinese vase, purity can be fully sensed only by those who pursue purity themselves, and this realization made my own sordid and tepid life seem small. While looking at the naked child and the Madonna's mysterious smile, I also realized that purity is a hidden and subtle virtue — a precious thing, available only to those who have been given the eyes to see.

But as soon as I speak the word *purity*, I'm aware of a certain sangfroid. Don't you curl up a little at the word? Like most people, I'm embarrassed and confused by the concept. I find that the mere word conjures up images of the "pure" girls of my youth who were all long skirts, buck teeth, and big Bibles. But when I saw true purity in the Raphael Madonna, I realized that, like many, I had confused purity with naiveté — the "aw shucks" innocence of Brylcreemed hair, bobbysocks, and bubble gum. We're rightly embarrassed by the false vision of purity exemplified by black-and-white TV programs where the married couples sleep in separate beds. This isn't purity in its primeval power. It is Pollyanna purity.

If we confuse purity with wholesome naiveté, we also confuse it with grim Puritanism: hatchet-faced nuns stalking the corridors of concentration-camp convent schools. When we hear "purity," we think of a squeaky-clean fundamentalist college with a sincere, but sinister agenda. This kind of "purity" points an accusing claw at all those sordid "sins against purity" which haunt the adolescent conscience. So instead of being an image of goodness, purity has been hijacked and twisted to become a tool of repression, guilt, and sour religion.

We also confuse purity with celestial otherworldliness. We think of Botticelli angels and entertain a vague notion of a lofty, unstained realm of existence where the saints and angels sit together in unimaginable and somewhat boring bliss. If we're really unlucky, our false religion mixes all three false images, so that the cruelty of Puritanism has a gloss of grinning Pollyanna along with the sentimentality of pink angels. The concept of purity has been so twisted in our modern minds that it almost doesn't exist.

And yet, when we say in the Creed that Jesus Christ was "born of the Virgin Mary," we're saying that he came into the world through a stupendous kind of purity that makes all our shallow concepts of purity look puerile. When we say in the Creed that Christ was "born of the Virgin Mary," we embrace the fact that in a Jewish girl in Nazareth two thousand years ago there existed a new matrix of purity and power, the likes of which hadn't been seen in the world since the dawn of time.

Mary, the mother of Jesus, is an icon of beauty and purity because she is a virgin. But I'm aware that this term, too, has been misunderstood and maligned. We think of a virgin simply as a person who hasn't had sexual intercourse. This is the shallowest of definitions. Defining a "virgin" as someone who hasn't had sexual intercourse is like defining a person from Idaho as "a person who has never been to Paris." It may be true that most Idahoans haven't been to Paris, but to define an untraveled Idahoan by that simple negative definition is too small. Even the most stay-at-home fellow from Idaho is bigger than a negative definition.

What were the early Christians thinking when they honored the Virgin Mary? Was it simply their form of goddess worship? If so, why the emphasis on virginity? When you look at what they believed about Mary, it turns out that they were honoring her for far more than the biological fact that a maiden remained intact. For them the Virgin wasn't just an untouched woman. Her physical virginity was a sign of something far more. It was an indication of her whole character. In her they sensed a kind of virginity that was a positive and powerful virtue. Mary represented all that was natural, abundant, positive, and free. Mary was a virgin in the same way that we call a forest "virgin": she was fresh and natural, majestic and mysterious. Mary's virginity wasn't simply the natural beauty and innocence of a teenage girl. It held the primeval purity of Eden and the awesome innocence of Eve.

This is precisely why the earliest theologians called the girl from Nazareth the "second Eve." The myth of the innocent first Mother evokes an image of Woman in all her primal power and radiant beauty. Eve was at once imperious and innocent, stupendous and simple. She was the Queen of Eden and the girl next door. If we were to meet Eve, we would meet a woman who held in herself the monumental innocence of nature — as majestic as a mountain and as tender as a rose. When the theologians of the second century called the Virgin Mary the "second Eve," they were also implying that, by a special act of God, she had been created without the fallen human tendency to choose evil. If this unique person didn't have the natural instinct to choose evil, then her will was unhindered and totally free. This freedom of choice burst into the darkened world to give humanity a second chance. In the primal Garden, the first woman said no to God and yes to herself. The girl of Nazareth gave humanity a chance to say no to itself and yes to God.

You might imagine that such total innocence and goodness would make Mary a sort of Galilean wonderwoman. It's true that her innocence was extraordinary, but it was also very ordinary. That is to say that while it was momentous, it didn't seem remarkable at the time. There is a curious twist to real goodness. It's summed up by the observation that what is natural isn't unusual. If a person is really good, he is humble; and if he is humble, he is simply who he should be. There is nothing bizarre or egotistical or eccentric about him. There is therefore nothing about him that calls attention to him. Truly good people blend in. They are at home with themselves, and no one is out of place when they are at home. In the same way, Mary wasn't noticed in Nazareth. Because she was natural, she didn't stand out. Mary fit in because she was simply and wholly who she was created to be. Because she was perfectly natural, she was perfectly ordinary. Therefore, she was both as marvelous and as unremarkable as a morning in May.

Meeting Mary may have been like seeing that Raphael Madonna. On the surface, it's a charming picture of a mother and child. Look more closely, and those who have eyes to see may just glimpse the magnitude and the mystery of God's becoming man through the womb of a woman. Likewise, meeting Mary may have been like meeting any other woman; and only those with the vision of a mystic would have sensed the extraordinary truth made manifest in this ordinary girl. This secret lies at the heart of Mary's purity, and it is this purity that makes her both invisible and invincible. This simple naturalness is the secret of her purity, and since she is pure, she is purely humble; and it is her simple humility that proves such a powerful secret weapon against the pride of the world.

In fact, her humility stands everything on its head. What is it that I live for? What is it that you live for? What is it that makes the whole world of power and commerce and politics turn? Day by day and moment by moment, our instinct is to live for ourselves and to do our own will. This drives everything and creates all the misery and suffering in the world. But what if there were a world where people didn't live for themselves, but lived to fit in with a greater order and a greater good? In that simple girl of Nazareth, a new way explodes into possibility. Not only was she humble, but a natural component of her humility was submissiveness. She said to God, "Let it be done to me as You say."[26] This is the fixed point of the fulcrum on which the world can be flipped over.

In our day, we howl at the mere idea that we ought to be submissive to anyone. To suggest that a woman be submissive is to express a heresy that makes you fit for burning. But let's stand that on its head. We assume that it's natural to be willful and to assert ourselves, but if there is a Creator, surely the natural thing is for all things to fit into their proper place in the created order. To do this, we must find our rightful place and be submissive to the natural order. Therefore, if Mary was as natural and innocent as a morning in May, she must have been submissive to God, because fitting ourselves into God's order is the natural, wholesome, and ordinary state for a human being. Looking at it that way, we find that it's prideful self-will which is strange and perverted — not submission.

Thus, Mary's response was revolutionary, for in a world of rebels, the one who submits is subversive. To prove how subversive she is, think about those Amish women who wear head coverings as a sign of their submission, or a nun who covers her head as a symbol of her vow of obedience. Aren't they shocking? Don't you instinctively recoil? Mary's total acceptance of God's will indicates the way not only for women, but also for men. In relationship to God, all of us are meant to be like Mary, and that is why Christians honor Mary more highly than any other creature.

The final twist is that purity and submission mean not impotence, but power. Purity is power because it aligns its own limited power in perfect harmony and cooperation with the one unlimited Power of the Universe. Mary's pure submission to the divine will points to possibilities for us. If we align ourselves perfectly to the greatest power that exists, we become agents of that power in the world in ways we could never expect. At the point of her submission, Mary heard the words, "With God nothing is impossible."[27] Notice the preposition. The phrase doesn't say, "*For* God nothing is impossible." We knew that already. Instead it says, "*With* God nothing is impossible." In other words, if you align yourself with God, you can do anything. At that point, Mary embraced the exhilarating and frightening reality that she lived in an open universe with everlasting and portentous potential; a universe where it's possible to align oneself with a will that is forever surprising and subversive; a will that is itself a magnificent and mighty blend of purity and power.

If we're able to comprehend the possibilities, we'll be stunned by the potential. But as soon as we're stunned by the potential, we realize that this submission is not only a possibility, but an imperative. Submission demands a choice. It doesn't happen on its own. C. S. Lewis observed that, at the end, there will be only two kinds of people: those who say, "Thy will be done" and those who say, "My will be done."[28] We have a choice between our will and God's will. We can choose all that is twisted and tiny and tainted, or we can choose all that is natural, enormous, and innocent. Like Eve and like Mary, we've been given free will. We can choose freedom, or we can choose slavery. We can limit ourselves to our own ever-narrowing will and enter a downward spiral of impurity and impotence; or we can align our will to the divine will and be caught up in an upward spiral of purity and power that has no boundaries and no natural end.

Chapter Seven

Agony and Agnosticism

. . . suffered under Pontius Pilate . . .

I nominate Pontius Pilate as patron saint of postmodernism. Like us, he lived in a sophisticated, multicultural society where different religions jostled for attention. He probably thought all religions had some goodness and truth to them. He probably thought they were all paths up the same mountain, and that each person had to choose the one that worked best for him.

In other words, Pilate was a practical agnostic. His agnosticism seemed urbane, tolerant, and practical, but his urbanity proved cruel, his tolerance allowed judicial murder, and his practicality turned out to be cowardice.

But if Pilate was a coward, he was also curious. No doubt he was sincere when he asked Jesus Christ, "What is truth?"[29] Pilate understood that truth is a slippery thing and that, while every man has some of the truth, no one has all of the truth. He may have been one of those who think the spirit of inquiry is more important than the spirit of truth. He may have had a poster on his wall with a path leading into the distance and the motto "To travel hopefully is better than to arrive."

Pilate asked Jesus, "What is truth?" but he did not see that Truth was standing right in front of him. Because of this blissful blindness, Pontius Pilate is the perfect patron of postmodernism. His blend of weary curiosity, cynicism, and careless agnosticism is a veritable portrait of our cynical and suspicious selves. His famous appeal to the opinion of the mob is the same sorry tyranny of the mob in our society — whether it's through the ballot box or market forces. Pilate's agnosticism is a sign of our times, but so is his agony. In a memorable play, Pontius Pilate is pictured in exile in his old age, still agonizing over his decision — or rather, his lack of decision. At that point, Pilate realizes that his worst choice was that he made no choice.

Because Pilate couldn't see the Truth when it stood in front of him, we sadly admit in the Creed that Jesus Christ "suffered under Pontius Pilate." He suffered not only by being tortured and killed; he suffered while he stood there waiting for Pilate's judgment. Anticipation is often worse than realization. Think of the tension as we await the result of a cancer test or the anxiety while a loved one undergoes the surgeon's knife. As much as he did at the pillar or upon the Cross, Christ suffered in meek, powerless silence while waiting for Pilate to decide what was to be done with him.

Christ continues to suffer at the hands of all those who suspend their judgment on him. We wish to view Jesus Christ at a dispassionate distance — as we would any other admirable martyr. But Christ will not be treated like Abraham Lincoln or Mahatma Gandhi or Martin Luther King, Jr. His life and his legacy are far more demanding. Of all historical figures, the evidence about Jesus Christ demands a verdict. He says plainly, "Follow me" and "He who is not with me is against me."[30]

Jesus Christ also said, "You cannot serve two masters."[31] Nor can you serve no master. In Bob Dylan's words, "You gotta serve somebody." Pilate's dilemma was indicative of our own. He wanted to wash his hands of Christ and get on with his career. But Pilate's choice was starker than he imagined. His choice wasn't between his career and Christ, but between Christ and Caligula. When Christ stood before him, Pilate was the servant of the emperor Tiberius, but waiting in the wings to step into his wicked uncle's big boots was the one known as "little boots" — or Caligula. Just a few years after Christ was crucified, Caligula became emperor. As the story of how Christ rose from the dead began to circulate among the slaves of the empire, the notorious beast Caligula rose to exercise his terrible tyranny. The legends tell us that when the mad teenager took the throne, Pilate was disgraced and sent into exile, where he eventually committed suicide.

Pilate's story is a parable for all practical agnostics. The grim moral of the story is that you can't avoid a choice. By not choosing, you *are* choosing. As it was for Pilate, the choice is between the Master of this world and the Master of the world to come. You must choose between Christ and Caligula, between the divine and the demonic, between the God-Man and the madman.

Pilate chose Caligula instead of Christ, but in an ironic quirk of history, both Christ and Caligula claimed to be an incarnate God. Jesus says, "I am Truth."[32] Caligula says, "I am Zeus." Isn't Pilate right to avoid such madness? It became clear that Caligula was a madman, but the disturbing thing about Christ is that, while he makes a mad claim, he seems to be one of the sanest people ever to walk the earth. Caligula was clearly both mad and bad, and this is proved by his actions. Christ also claims to be God incarnate, but by his actions, it seems he is neither mad nor bad. On the contrary, he seems to be the most whole and holy person who ever lived.

Jesus doesn't claim to speak the truth, as any good teacher may do. He claims to *be* the Truth. This is the claim that demands a decision. There are only three choices. When he says, "I am the Truth," either the claim is true or false. If it's false, he is either a maniac like Caligula, or he is a liar (in which case, he is not a good teacher). The only other option is that his claim is true. If he is indeed the Truth, he demands our total allegiance and the service of our whole life.

Pilate's response in the face of this person is the response most of us make. We wish to sit on the fence. We wish to withhold judgment. We refer it to a majority vote so we don't have to take the responsibility to decide ourselves. We push the question away and claim agnosticism as our refuge. But the hound of Heaven sniffs us out, and our agnosticism soon becomes, not an ecstasy, but an agony.

Agnosticism becomes an agony because the greatest questions of life demand an answer, as a lover demands a commitment. Christianity, like life, demands that we make decisions. It demands that we use our will. It demands involvement. Not to choose is itself a choice. When a bus comes along, you can choose to get on the bus, or you can choose not to get on the bus. Making "no choice" amounts to choosing to stay off.

You may quite fairly say that you don't know whether the bus is going to the right destination and choose to wait for the next one; but that, too, is a choice not to get on the bus. You may quite fairly say that you're uncertain as to the safety claims of the bus company and that you're withholding judgment for the time being; but that, too, is a choice not to get on the bus. According to the nature of choice, therefore, agnosticism is an illusion. It's wishful thinking. Like Pilate's washing his hands of the whole matter, it's simply a stage gesture — an act that convinces only the actor.

The honest agnostic may come back with the reply, "I simply don't know." But what doesn't he know that believers do know? If he has explored religion and the claims of Jesus Christ, he has as much knowledge about the Christian Faith as most people do, and many people decide to set out on the adventure of faith based on that limited knowledge. Therefore, when the agnostic pleads that he "doesn't know" whether there is a God or whether Jesus Christ is the Savior of the World, he's simply admitting what many good Christians would admit to as well. Neither do they know for sure that there is a God and that Jesus is his Son.

There are different kinds of knowing. I knew enough about my wife to get married. I now know far more about her, and she (to her chagrin) knows far more about me. In the marriage commitment comes a new kind of knowing that can't be had on the other side of marriage. Within marriage there's a kind of human sacrifice. (That's why we say a man is being led to the altar.) In this mutual sacrifice of commitment, one enters into a new and frightening kind of knowledge, and it's the same with religious faith. There's plenty of astounding evidence, but in the end a leap of faith is required. You can take skydiving lessons, study aerodynamics, learn how to fold a parachute, and enter an airplane. You can put on a helmet and a parachute and stand at the door, but you still won't know what skydiving is like. There comes a point when you have to jump.

Faith is a terrible and exciting gamble. Living by faith means living life with a passionate purpose and a heart on fire. Real faith requires a terrifying moment of self-surrender. By comparison, agnosticism is so safe and timid. But agnosticism's apparent safety is like the safety of staying on a sinking ship. Faith jumps for the life raft and swims for safety — or drowns in the attempt. It's no coincidence that the arch-agnostic Pontius Pilate committed suicide, for agnosticism is the view that we can't know whether there's something worth living for, and if there's nothing worth living for, why go on living?

The life of faith, on the other hand, is a come-Hell-or-high-water adventure. It's true that some religious people have turned the life of faith into a spectator sport. It's as if they mistake watching ski jumping on television for actually putting on skis and taking off down the ramp. But because religion has become dull for some doesn't negate the fact that faith is a vibrant option for others. There are real ski jumpers out there, and there's a real chance to live rather than merely to watch others live.

Christ can be contrasted with Caligula, but Pilate must be compared with Peter. Pilate washed his hands in a ceremony of detachment. Peter cries out to Jesus, "Do not wash just my feet, but wash me all over!"[33] Pilate is dispassionate, while Peter is passionate. Pilate seems wise in his detached deference to reason. Peter plays the unreasonable fool time and again. Consider how he steps out of the boat on a stormy night to take the walk of faith. He rocks and reels as he walks on the water, then finally starts to sink. Like Pilate, the detached agnostic remains safely in the boat and decides to ride out the storm. Like Peter, the person of faith steps out and walks forward into a world as uncertain as the waves and the wind — a world that opens onto unexpected and perplexing possibilities.

Chapter Eight

I Scream, Therefore I Am

. . . was crucified, died, and was buried . . .

When my nephew Michael was getting ready for college, he told me he was expected to write a paper in his first week entitled, "How do I know I exist?" After discussing the matter for some time, he concluded that the best thing to do was to punch his professor in the nose. The resulting pain when the professor punched back would thereby prove that both of them existed.

Michael was unusual for a college freshman. Like anyone who has wondered whether things continue to be there once you stop looking at them, Michael wondered whether in some way the existence of everything was linked with his own existence: if he didn't exist, then maybe nothing else did either. To get some answers, he had been snooping through some basic philosophy books and came across René Descartes' memorable sound bite, "I think, therefore I am." Michael found it unconvincing, but wasn't sure why. Descartes thought the fact that he was aware of the activity of his mind proved his existence. For Descartes, thinking wasn't just a matter of logic or figuring out his tax return. It included the whole range of mental activity like emotions and the experience of pleasure and pain. Despite all his doubts and uncertainty, he was at least certain that he was thinking, and that made him conclude that he existed.

But is there anything outside our own thought with which we can make contact to validate our existence? What about that lift of the mind and heart when I view a beautiful person, a Raphael Madonna, or a breathtaking landscape? Does the experience of aesthetic pleasure prove I exist? It certainly hints at something greater than ourselves, but pleasure is notoriously fickle. What pleases one may cause revulsion to another. At times pleasure may point us toward an objective existence outside ourselves, but that process is unreliable because it's often unrepeatable. We return to that same mountaintop to experience that same sunset which was so sublime, but all we see is the sun disappearing below the hills, so we decide to sit down and eat a sandwich instead. The Man from Missouri will point out that what we experience as pleasure is also just a series of chemical reactions. So if our senses and our experience of pleasure can't validate our existence, what can?

Fed up with such pointless speculation, Samuel Johnson famously kicked a stone to prove that he was real. But what was it about kicking the stone that convinced Dr. Johnson that he existed? Would he have been as convinced if he had kissed the stone and not kicked it? I doubt it. It wasn't only the solidity of the stone, but also the nerve endings in his toes that convinced him that he and the stone both existed. In other words, pain proves our existence. As he hops around on one foot, Dr. Johnson tops Descartes with a new proof of human existence. Between his gasps of pain, he might have also gasped, "I scream, therefore I am!"

Could it be that pain is the ultimate proof of our existence? The Man from Missouri will step in at this point to remind us that pain, too, is merely a sensation of the brain and therefore only a chemical reaction. But pain is different from the other sensations that the brain interprets. First, pain is the most intense sensation of all. We know that pleasure feels good, but we really know that pain feels bad. Even the most pleasurable experience isn't as good as having a tooth pulled out is bad. Furthermore, pain is always intense, whereas pleasure suffers from the law of diminishing returns. The second chocolate bar isn't as good as the first, but the second pulled tooth is just as bad or worse than the first.

Second, sensual information and the experience of pleasure are mixed with a mass of data in our brains that causes us to interpret the sensations in subtle and subjective ways, and this process permits all sorts of unreliable conclusions. So, for instance, the physical pleasure of being kissed is mixed with our feelings for the person doing the kissing, our moral framework, and the complexity of sexual arousal. All of this complicates and confuses the simple pleasure of kissing. Pain, on the other hand, is simple, raw data. Pain is not subtle. It's sharply negative and can't be ignored or misinterpreted. Even a masochist winces before he sighs.

Third, have you noticed how pain is always surprising? Even when we know something is going to hurt, the pain comes as a shock. It leads to numbness and a sense of unreality. The sudden amputee looks at his severed hand and doesn't believe it's his. This shocking sense of unreality reinforces the surprising aspect of pain. The fact that we scream, "This can't be happening to me!" leads to the conclusion that it's an authentic experience, because we wouldn't be surprised and shocked by something we devised or desired for ourselves. Therefore, pain validates my own experience because it clearly comes from outside myself. My desire for pleasure or information leads me to pursue pleasurable and interesting stimuli, but that pleasure and information can't prove my existence, because I pursued it and thus I was biased. I wanted a particular thing to be pleasurable or to give me information. In contrast, pain is an interloper. It's something I don't seek. It's a shocking surprise. It invades my life, and it hurts. Pain is a little morsel of objective truth and therefore is the most accurate proof of my existence. If it's true that pain proves my existence, then the old saying, "Truth hurts," is true in far deeper ways than we thought.

Pain also validates our existence, because, unlike pleasure, pain isn't fickle. Different brains treat pleasurable stimuli in different ways. The sunset that gives you pleasure may cause me to yawn. The opera that I find thrilling you may find killing. I like broccoli, but you can eat it only with cheese sauce. Taste makes pleasure subjective and ephemeral, but when all of us kick a stone, all of us dance with pain and thus prove, not only our own experience, but our shared existence. Similarly, the effect of pain is more repeatable than pleasure. Your fourth bowl of ice cream will never taste as good as the first, but kick a stone repeatedly, and you'll find each pang in your toe as vivid as any other. Thus, pain is the most reliable, fixed, and authentic proof of our existence.

Pleasure is more likely to anesthetize the soul, but pain is the pinch that wakes us up. What makes us face the largest and most dangerous questions of life? Sometimes pleasure, but more often pain. Someone is diagnosed with cancer, or we cling to the precipice of life after an accident, or a car knocks down our child. Then, in the terror and tremendous pain, we know beyond a shadow of a doubt that we exist. There, in the screaming darkness, we understand that we are alive, even if we wish we were dead.

Pain proves our existence in a negative way. It screams out to us that something is missing. Something is wrong. Things aren't as they should be. Pain is very powerful, but it isn't positive. It's real, but it isn't reality. Pain is like a shadow. As a shadow proves the existence of the object that casts the shadow, so pain proves our existence. But a shadow not only proves the existence of the object that casts the shadow; it also proves the existence of light. Light is the positive quality that, by default, produces shadow. Likewise pain, because it is negative, tells us not only that we exist, but that there must be such a thing as an existence without pain. In the same way, hunger and thirst not only prove the existence of our stomach; they demand the existence of food and drink.

If all this is true, then my nephew's conclusion that he should punch his professor in the nose was deeply meaningful. I think, therefore I am? No. I scream, therefore I am. Once this proposition is put into the context of Christian belief, it becomes apparent why Jesus Christ is called a "man of sorrows and acquainted with grief."[34] You could rephrase it and say because he was a man, he had sorrows and was acquainted with grief. If pain is at the heart of our humanity, and if God was going to take human form, then it makes sense that the God-Man would have intense pain at the very core of his experience.

This is why Christians have crucifixes in all their churches: they prove that all of us exist. The climax of Jesus Christ's human existence was the excruciating reality of crucifixion. Not only was Jesus Christ's Crucifixion physically painful; it was also psychological torment. On the Cross, a person everyone admitted was good and wise was killed as a criminal. The suffering seemed senseless. It was absurd, and this is surely the most terrible thing about suffering. No one objects too much when a wicked person dies a long and painful death, but when a little child is abused, murdered, dismembered, and thrown into a ditch, all of us scream with fury and grief at the insane and terrifying evil of such a deed. In the face of such absurd horror, we shake our fist and ask, "Why?" But there is no answer. The sheer mindlessness of this kind of evil is exactly why it's evil. The cruel suffering of an innocent victim hurts most because it's absurd. And it's at this point of soul-searing cosmic anguish that all humanity is most acutely, authentically and awfully alive.

Suffering is not only the proof of our existence; it's also the turning point of the whole drama of why we're here at all. In the face of innocent suffering, Jesus Christ didn't deliver a neat philosophical discourse on suffering. He didn't expound a spiritual method that would provide an escape route from suffering. Instead, in a most awesome, tragic, and dramatic action, Christ embraced suffering and went through it. This is what we mean when we say that his death was redemptive: he introduced the possibility that suffering itself could be a redemptive transaction. He did this not with words, but with action. He accepted his sentence and went to an absurd, agonizing, and humiliating death. Then, at the darkest moment, he proclaimed the most eloquent and moving sermon on suffering ever preached, by crying, "It is finished!"[35]

When examining any religion, we must examine how it deals with this problem of suffering. By his example on the Cross, Christ shows us the authentic Christian way. Buddhism seeks to forget suffering and rise above it. Primitive religions offer sacrifices to gods who promise to deliver the devotee from suffering. Indeed, certain forms of Christianity also make this false promise. But they're wrong. Jesus Christ showed a new way. To be authentically human, to be really alive, to know we exist most fully, we have to scream. We have to go through suffering — not around it or over it. That's what Christ meant when he said, "If any man would be my disciple, he must take up his cross and follow me."[36]

Jesus realized that to be authentically human, we can't avoid suffering. Doesn't the fact that we came into the world howling and will leave it whimpering suggest the same grim truth? Suffering is at the core of our existence. No one can suffer for us. We have to face it. We are sick, and we have to go through the surgery of suffering in order to be healed. Jesus suffers and dies, not to deliver us out of suffering, but to deliver us through suffering. He shows us that the only way to cope with suffering is to wrestle with it and pull a reversal. Christianity calls us to win a victory, not to run from the fight.

The Christian life isn't about picking spiritual posies and feeling happy in Jesus. It's about establishing a mysterious bond with this most mysterious of men. In a strange and symbiotic relationship, the Christian claims to plunge into the stark reality of Christ's Crucifixion. He does this through the mysterious rituals of his religion and through the mundane rituals of his own human suffering. In that crushing process, the ordinary Christian begins to find redemption and release. The salvation Christians talk about is therefore not an all-expenses-paid excursion to Heaven. It's a summons to battle and the invitation to risk all to share in the victory over evil.

Seeing salvation as the final holiday in Heaven has made Christianity into a sentimental nonsense. Many people see Christianity as greeting card religion. They perceive it as a sentimental escape route from reality. In fact, it's an expressway into reality.

It's true that many Christians use Christianity as a cozy cop-out, but for every hundred who do, there are ten like Mother Teresa or the old priest in the next-door parish who realize that at the heart of Christianity is the stark fact of the Crucifixion of Jesus Christ.

That absurd torture at the core of the Christian Faith forces them to confront the reality of human existence. As these authentic Christians take on the burden of suffering, they enter a new dimension of human reality — a dimension of life where every detail is as hard and beautiful as diamonds; a dimension where they find divine power hidden in frailty and a tender humility that is radiant with glory.

Chapter Nine

Out of the Frying Pan

He descended into hell . . .

Someone once asked the famous mystic-saint Padre Pio what he thought of modern people who didn't believe in Hell. His terse reply was "They will believe in Hell when they get there."

Is it possible to believe in Hell? Surely, when faced with Auschwitz, the Gulag, and the killing fields of Cambodia, the question should be "Is it possible *not* to believe in Hell?" I don't simply refer to the fact that concentration camps were a kind of hell on earth. Instead I wonder how one can deny the existence of a place of final punishment when faced with Hitler, Stalin, Pol Pot, and African soldiers who chop off little girls' hands for fun. When faced with such monsters, can we really cry with a good conscience, "God would not send anyone to burn forever in the fires of everlasting torment!"? After a century that has witnessed more genocide, religious martyrdom, and brutality to children than ever before in human history, can we really dismiss the only punishment left for the dictators, terrorist bombers, and genocidal maniacs who have gotten away with their crimes? If it were true that there is no Hell, I, for one, would be howling with rage at the insanity and unfairness of it all. Yet those who deny the existence of Hell think that their denial shows how enlightened and humane (and therefore fair) they are.

These are good people. They dismiss the possibility of Hell, not because they deny the wickedness of human beings, but because they affirm the goodness of God. They believe in a God who is so very good that he would not send anyone to Hell.

It would certainly be nice if there were a Heaven but not a Hell. But can you believe in one without the other? What I mean is, how can someone believe in Heaven, a place of goodness (and if goodness, then justice), while denying the fact of Hell, which makes justice possible? It seems to me that if you believe in Heaven, you must also believe in Hell. Hell is somehow written into the constitution of Heaven.

Nevertheless, good-hearted people insist that a good God wouldn't send anyone to be tormented in Hell for all eternity. This is a laudable sentiment, but I sometimes worry that it's nothing more than sentimental. Even so, the conviction that God wouldn't send anyone to Hell is a feeling I myself incline to — especially after a warm day in June followed by a very good dinner with several glasses of claret. Furthermore, at that moment, I'm not usually thinking about Pol Pot or Stalin. I'm thinking that God wouldn't send an ordinary, decent fellow like me to Hell.

But this is exactly the point where the possibility of Hell is meant to knock me down and shake me up. We are told that the road to Hell is a wide, smooth, downhill highway, while the road to Heaven is a mountainous climb, narrow and hard. What if Hell were populated with hordes of overweight, complacent people just like me who never really did anything magnificently evil, but also never bothered to do anything spectacularly good? Is it possible that Hell is reserved for the mediocre?

When I look at it this way, and knowing my own mediocrity, I have the dreadful suspicion that perhaps those who deny Hell because God is too good to send anyone there are really proposing that God is too good to send *them* there. It's ironic that people who believe in Heaven are sometimes blamed for wishful thinking. Isn't it more likely that those who disbelieve in Hell are the wishful thinkers? I say this because the person who disbelieves in Hell doesn't really believe in Heaven either. He believes in oblivion. He desperately hopes that he'll cease to exist after death. He hopes he'll get away with it after all, and this, it seems to me, is real wishful thinking.

Others protest that the concept of eternal punishment makes God out to be an angry, short-tempered disciplinarian of the worst sort. But is God such a nice, middle-class English gentleman that he wouldn't be angry enough to send anyone to Hell? What if God were more like a passionate and hot-tempered Mediterranean papa?

That isn't to say that God is petulant and petty. He isn't angry with wickedness the way our fifteen-year-old is angry when he refuses to tidy his room. God doesn't slam the door and stamp his foot. Neither is God angry the way we are when we don't get our way. He doesn't sulk, give the silent treatment, and pretend nothing is wrong. If God is angry with the wicked, it isn't because he is an arbitrary and babyish tyrant who loses his temper when he is disobeyed.

What if, instead, God's anger is of the sort we feel when we hear of a young boy being abducted, abused, killed, and dumped in a ditch? What if God's anger is the sort of anger and revulsion you feel when you watch the news and see a young African woman whose hands have been cut off by rampaging soldiers, leaving her unable to cuddle the child those same soldiers gave her when they raped her? What if God's anger is the disgust you feel when you hear of a middle-aged Barbie clone who has paid millions for plastic surgery in a world of starving children? When you hear such news, don't you respond with an element of rage as well as disbelief, horror, and grief? Aren't you righteous to do so? And if God is infinitely more righteous than we are, might not his rage be something too terrible to imagine? Perhaps God is angry at the wicked in the same way we are when we witness such horrors. He sees the everlasting beauty and goodness of his creation, and when it is soiled, trampled, raped, and burned by humanity's greed and stupidity, he is filled with a rage mixed with frustration, sorrow, and compassion.

But does that mean God would cast someone into Hell to be tortured forever? Perhaps this question, too, can be looked at upside down: Is God too good to send someone to Hell?

It could be that God is so good that he actually gives people exactly what they want. If we have spent our whole lives pursuing love, goodness, beauty, and truth, then after death we may get exactly what we always wanted and find ourselves in a land where love, goodness, beauty, and truth are as natural and abundant as light. On the other hand, if we spend our whole lives in an insane flight from all that is good, beautiful, and true, then perhaps God in his goodness will also give us exactly what we always wanted: existence in a madhouse with no exit, where love, beauty, goodness, and truth are unknown; an eternity in the outer darkness with gibbering maniacs like ourselves.

Life pans out, and despite our greatest efforts, we almost always end up getting what we really want. In fact, this sort of justice is built into the system. We will get what we want just as naturally and certainly as an acorn becomes an oak tree. Giving people what they really want is natural justice. To do otherwise would be cruel and arbitrary. We think everyone ought to go to Heaven, but can we imagine that a person who hated God all his life would actually enjoy Heaven? If he could visit that place of eternal beauty and laughter, he would howl with serious terror and run with all his might in the other direction. We know this is true because there are people in this life who hate truth, beauty, and goodness and do everything in their power either to flee from the light or to put out the light forever. If this is so, then perhaps Hell is built into the very fabric of Heaven; the same blinding radiance that for some is the burning light of life will for others be the burning fires of death.

Is Hell a real place? Now, this is where the topic really starts to interest me. Down through the ages, human beings from every culture and time have recorded fascinating stories about their visits to Hell. I wish I could recount them because they are far more fun and interesting than philosophical speculation on the topic.

Here is one story: The philosopher A. J. Ayer (a noted atheist) choked on a piece of smoked salmon one day. His heart stopped for four minutes before he was revived. When he came back, he recounted his experience. His biographer writes, "He had been confronted by a bright red light, painful even when he turned away from it, which he understood to be responsible for the government of the universe. . . . Ayer became more and more desperate. . . . [W]hen he regained consciousness, he spoke about crossing a river — presumably the river Styx — which he claimed to have crossed."[37] In subsequent interviews, Ayer admitted that the experience had made him feel "wobbly," but he soon reverted to type and labeled himself as a "born-again atheist."

Witches, exorcists, and mediums tell us how they have summoned or wrestled against demons. The visionaries of Marian apparitions have been given glimpses of Hell. One of the visionaries of Fatima described the sight:

> The rays of light seemed to penetrate the earth, and we saw, as it were, a sea of fire. Plunged in this fire were demons and souls in human form, like transparent burning embers, all blackened or burnished bronze floating about in the conflagration, now raised into the air by the flames that issued from within themselves together with great clouds of smoke, now falling back on every side like sparks in huge fires, without weight or equilibrium, amid shrieks and groans of pain and despair. . . . [T]he demons could be distinguished by their terrifying and repellent likeness to frightful and unknown animals, black and transparent like burning coals.[38]

This is literally hot stuff. This is jalapeño religion — green, hot, mouth- and eye-watering religion. These are the sort of outrageous religious experiences you want to bring up in that circle of educated and urbane religious folks just to see their politely horrified reaction. Don't you think that real religion ought to feature juicy bits like this? In fact, it could almost be the test of real religion: that it have visions and horrifying encounters with the supernatural. Any religion that weeds out such stuff due to good taste or fashionable incredulity isn't a religion at all; it's a set of table manners.

These visions of Hell and devils don't make for happy bedtime reading — especially if your bed happens to be a deathbed. Despite my delight with such visions, I realize that mystical visions and near-death experiences don't constitute proof for the existence of Hell. But they do point to a universal strain in human consciousness, for practically every religion and culture perpetuates similar stories of human visitors who return from the underworld with horrific tales of justice for the wicked. The person who denies Hell is therefore the outsider and the renegade — not the person who affirms it.

The question remains open, and if it remains open, then I know which way I'd wager. Suddenly, believing in Heaven and Hell isn't wishful thinking at all. It's prudent — as prudent as a second parachute or a life-insurance policy.

Those who believe in Hell are often blamed for being self-righteous. It's imagined that one can only believe in Hell for one's enemies. But the Christian position on Hell is quite plain — to the point of being impolite. The Christian preacher delivers a simple two-word sermon on the subject — "Fear Hell" — and if the preacher tells others to fear Hell, he must fear it himself. I realize this may be too crude for those of delicate religious sensibilities. Some will complain that such sermons get people into Heaven only by scaring them out of Hell. There are certainly more noble reasons for desiring Heaven, but none more effective. I admit that I'm human. I'm scared of monsters, demons, and death, pitchforks and pain, and if there are such places as Heaven and Hell, I, for one, would rather be scared into Heaven than soothed into Hell. Is my vision of Heaven and Hell too literal? I would rather discover one day that my vision of Hell was too literal than discover that it was not literal enough.

If such a place exists why did Jesus Christ go there?

We say Christ "descended into hell," but this doesn't mean he waded through eternal lakes of fire bubbling with eternally tortured souls. Before Christ came, it was impossible to accept or reject him; therefore the final torment of rejecting him couldn't yet exist. At that stage, Hell wasn't the land of the damned, but simply the land of the dead — a kind of gloomy waiting room for all those who hadn't yet been given the light. In these shadow-lands, there were two sorts of people: those who would accept Christ if they could, and those who would accept anything but Christ. Before they could make their choice, Christ had to be made known to them, and what better way to send a message than personal delivery?

So when Christ went to the realm of the dead, he accomplished three things: First, by his appearance, those who had rejected all that he stood for would confirm their choice and run from him further into the everlasting darkness. Others, in seeing him, would recognize their beloved, the truth they had always sought. In their case, his arrival would have opened the door to Paradise. Finally, his faithful friends from the ages before his coming were waiting, like marooned sailors, to be rescued.

Jesus went down to rescue his friends, but did he also go to rescue his enemies?

Certainly the tradition is that once he died on the Cross, Jesus descended into the underworld like Orpheus to find and rescue his loved ones. The tradition also says that he went to preach to them. This poignant possibility is put most simply by a child who was receiving religious instruction. The priest asked the question "Where did Jesus go after he had died on the Cross?" The little boy sat and pondered the question for some time. Eventually he put his face in his hands. After a long pause he looked up with an expression of sorrow on his face and said with great solemnity, "I think he went down to the deepest, darkest corner of Hell to look for his friend Judas."

If this is so, then the reality of Hell is burst wide open in an astounding way. If Christ descended into Hell, then his Incarnation really begins to make sense. If descent to rescue the lowest is part of his humble nature, then going down even to the place of the dead might be the final step in the spiraling staircase Christ started down when he was born in that cave in Bethlehem.

This habit of descent is an integral and mysterious part of who Christ really is. While it is his nature to establish a justice that can't avoid Hell, perhaps it's also his nature to establish a justice that always seeks to save us from Hell. It would be comforting to hope that his constant search for the lost might extend for all time. It would be beautiful to hope that part of the everlasting justice is an everlasting mercy, and that until the end of time Christ will be throwing down a lifeline — hoping that someone down there might just give it a tug.

But such a hope neglects the stark nature of choice. Those who reject life, love, and light have not made a static decision. They are not standing still. They have chosen to travel down a particular road to a particular destination. They are continuing down that road, and like any journey, the further you go, the more difficult it is to turn back, until at last it's impossible to turn back. The horrible truth is that those who choose to run from the light in this life, will run from the light forever.

Chapter Ten

Memes, Magicians, and Manichees

. . . on the third day rose again.

Some years ago, there was an Anglican bishop who was asked his opinion about the Christian belief that Jesus Christ rose from the dead on the third day. The bishop said he believed in the Resurrection, but not in any crude physical way. "The Resurrection," he stated, "was not a conjuring trick with bones."

This was a conjuring trick with words. The bishop, like many modern theologians, was an expert at verbal legerdemain. What the bishop meant was that he believed in the Resurrection, but not the physical Resurrection.

I hope the bishop was saying the Resurrection was more than a conjuring trick with bones, but I fear he was simply saying that it didn't really happen, that the Resurrection account was just a lovely story with a nice meaning. Many modern clergymen and -women understand the Resurrection in this way. So on Easter Day, Reverend Mandrake will stand in the pulpit and proclaim, "Today we celebrate the glorious Resurrection of our Lord Jesus Christ from the dead." What he means is, "In some wonderful way, the teachings of Jesus were remembered by his disciples after he was dead."

However, what Mrs. Bloggins in the front row thinks he means is that he believes that Jesus' body was brought back to life miraculously; that his disciples saw it, put their fingers in the nail holes, and watched him eat a breakfast of broiled fish and toast. With this verbal trick, the Reverend is able to please both Mrs. Bloggins and the bishop. In other words, he is able to fool everybody — even himself.

A plain-thinking person might be excused for distrusting the clergyman. "He has said one thing, but means another!" The ordinary fellow in the street thus puts the modern clergyman in the same category as the politician, the used-car salesman, and the snake-oil shyster. It's easy to criticize this clergyman for being dishonest, but we must forgive him. Like the naked emperor's courtiers, he only believed what he had been told to believe. Furthermore, the modernist bishop and his clergy sincerely believe that by saying one thing and meaning another in this way, they are being more honest. So the bishop might say, "I'm not so naive or literal in my understanding as to expect Jesus physically to rise from the dead. Surely the true meaning of this belief is that he continued to exist in some spiritual manner."

The problem is the old either-or dilemma. Those who deny the physical Resurrection assume that those who believe in it must be so dumbly awe-struck by the miracle that they miss its spiritual meaning. But stand on your head, and you'll see that the spiritual meaning of the Resurrection is dependent on the physical event. It's the physical fact of the Resurrection that makes the spiritual aspect jump up and dance a joyful jig.

Anyway, aren't you suspicious of any theory that's all "spiritual"? It's too ethereal and otherworldly. Any religion that "spiritualizes" away the physical aspect betrays a negative attitude toward it. This attitude was made famous by a third-century thinker called Manichaeus. His followers were called Manichees, which makes them sound like a cross between a sea cow and a Chinese fruit. Despite the strange name, they believed something that's very easy to believe: that the physical is filthy and vulgar and nasty, while the spiritual is clean and ethereal and nice. But I'm suspicious of things that are easy to believe. If they're easy to believe, it's all too likely that they're comfortable; and if they're comfortable, they're probably not true.

Manichaeus concluded that the physical was inferior, because he thought that Satan had stolen particles of light from the world of Light and imprisoned them in man's brain. The object of religion was to liberate these particles of light from their sordid physical captivity. The way to release the light imprisoned in the brain was to suppress the physical realm through extreme asceticism. I doubt that the Anglican bishop I mentioned was a Manichee in that respect; in fact, he was plump and somewhat of a bon vivant. I can hardly imagine him sacrificing his dining rights at high table to sit in a snowdrift in his underpants in order to liberate the particles of light from his brain. However, inasmuch as he found the physical Resurrection of Jesus to be distasteful, he was a Manichee.

I use the word *distasteful* because I suspect that educated and sophisticated people deny physical miracles, not so much because they're incredible, but because they're an error in taste. Physical miracles are embarrassing. There's something subversive and unpredictable about them. However, the fear of being embarrassed is itself an embarrassing thing to admit, so they devise intellectual reasons for not believing in the miraculous. The most famous foundation for this denial is the philosophy of David Hume, who simply asserted that miracles are impossible because miracles can't happen.[39] This bald statement is then taken as a watertight philosophical conclusion.

It seems leaky to me.

Hume assumed that the physical universe ran like a clock according to fixed and unalterable principles. Therefore, miracles were impossible if they contradicted these principles. If something seemed to be miraculous, it was simply because we hadn't yet figured out how it fit into the machine of the cosmos. But if the universe is actually expanding, as we now think, doesn't that suggest that it isn't quite so fixed as we thought? Perhaps the cosmos is more like rubber than like concrete. If so, the unpredictable is possible, and strange things can happen. If the universe is elastic, maybe miracles aren't an aberration from the natural order. Rather, they might well be an ordinary, but unpredictable part of it. The universe might be more like a party than like a stage play.

Perhaps, then, God is a God of surprises; a God who likes tricks, twists in the tail, paradoxes, and unexpected pleasures. Miracles, especially the Resurrection of Jesus Christ, are just that sort of reversal we'd expect from a good storyteller. The hero descends to the deepest depth, and at that point he turns the plot, twists the knife, and rises to triumph. Now, the historical, physical, miraculous event of the Resurrection certainly has much spiritual significance, but if you reduce it totally to spiritual significance, doesn't that rob it of the very significance you wish to give it?

Saying you believe in the Resurrection only in "a spiritual sense" is not to believe in the Resurrection at all, because the whole (astounding and scandalous) point of the Resurrection is that it was physical. Two thousand years ago, hundreds of witnesses reported seeing a man alive whom three days before they had seen tortured to death. The witnesses reported being frightened out of their wits. They thought he was an apparition or a ghost, but then they saw him eat fish and bread. They touched him and put their fingers in his oozing wounds.

This isn't what happens when something is true in a spiritual sense. When something is true in a spiritual sense, bishops discuss it with their clergy over a glass of dry sherry. When something is true in a spiritual sense, old ladies mutter together around crystal balls and packs of Tarot cards. When something is true in a spiritual sense, people sit with their legs crossed and hum Hindi words together.

But when something like the Resurrection is true, utterly and physically true, people are scared. They run and weep and cry out in fear. Then, once they have grasped the reality of the event, they get on and do something. They don't do something "in a spiritual sense"; they do something real and physical and world-changing.

This is precisely what happened after the Resurrection of Jesus Christ. Twelve working-class men who were hiding for fear of their lives suddenly became the nucleus of a force that changed the world forever. Something must have happened, and it wasn't simply that "in some wonderful, spiritual way the teachings of their friends continued to echo in their minds and spread around the world." This theory reminds me of a fascinating idea of Professor Dawkins. He suggests that there is such a thing as a "meme": a brain particle that transfers its knowledge to another person's brain by some mysterious power. Through the mechanism of memes, dead people can seem to live in a vivid way even after they're dead, and their ideas may spread after they die. This is an interesting concept, and some people have found it a beautiful way to think of Jesus Christ's Resurrection.

But the Resurrection of Jesus Christ from the dead is far more than either a memory or a meme. Those of us who believe freely admit that the event is embarrassingly physical — even to the extent of being vulgar. We think it really happened. We believe that it's a physical, historical, and actual fact, like the assassination of

JFK or the coronation of Queen Elizabeth. Furthermore, some of us are delighted to believe that there exists a photograph of the actual moment. We theorize that the darkness of the tomb acted like the inside of a camera, and the radiance of that Resurrection burned Jesus' physical features into the inside of his shroud, and that you can see the snapshot of the event to this day in the cathedral in Turin.

Of course the Resurrection is an astounding miracle. It's a unique event, but, then, that is the definition of a miracle — it's an unpredictable blip in the normal day-to-day running of things. From an everyday point of view, the Resurrection seems incredible, but if you accept the primary doctrine of the Christian Faith — that Jesus is God in human form — then the Resurrection is not so surprising at all. If Jesus really is a unique synthesis of divinity and humanity, wouldn't you expect something unique to happen when he died? If he really is the God-Man, would you expect him to stay dead?

Belief in the physical Resurrection is actually crucial to the whole Christian Faith, because Christianity is about the real possibility of a new kind of human existence. Jesus rose from the dead simply because there was nothing dead about him. In other words, because there was nothing decaying and impure about him, he couldn't stay dead. His life was so dynamic, vital, and pure that it simply had to come back again. His life could not be killed forever. Instead, it bursts from the darkness of death with a life that is, not less real, but more real than what we had come to expect. The Resurrection of Jesus Christ comes trumpeting in with its blatant physical-ness, as something, not unnatural, but more natural than we could have imagined. His Resurrection says, "What you thought was life is a pallid reflection of life. See this resurrected body? This is what life is."

That's why he said he came: "to give life in all its abundance."[40] This doesn't simply mean he came to give everyone a happy life; it means he came to give life itself — which by definition is the opposite of death. He offers this life to all those who wish to accept it. It's a gift, and like any gift, it must be either accepted or rejected.

Faith accepts the gift, but to ignore it is just another way of rejecting it. Turning the Resurrection of Jesus Christ into a merely "spiritual" truth is also a way of rejecting it; a very subtle and refined rejection, mind you — like quietly throwing away a diamond ring while keeping the pretty box.

Softening the scandal of the Resurrection by turning it into a "spiritual truth" won't do, simply because by its very nature it can't be merely a "spiritual" truth. By definition it's a historical, physical event, and the documents of the early Church are written to express this unpalatable and socially awkward fact. This is why the first Christian theologian said in a most astringent manner, "If the Resurrection did not happen, then our faith is in vain."[41]

In other words, "If this isn't true, then the rest of it isn't either." Let's not mince words and go all gooey and spiritual. Billions of people for the last two thousand years believe that this astounding miracle really took place in a backwater of the Roman Empire around the year 33 A.D. Either it happened or it didn't. If you don't believe it, why, then, eat, drink, and be merry, for tomorrow you die. But please don't spiritualize the whole thing. That is not one of the options.

Chapter Eleven

Up, Up, and Away

He ascended into Heaven . . .

Those who accuse Christianity of being a fairytale have some good ammunition when it comes to the Ascension of Jesus Christ into Heaven. Doesn't it sound like the perfect fairytale ending? Jesus stands on a hillside and says goodbye to his friends, then floats up into the sky. Angels appear to tell his friends not to be too sad because he will come again one day. It's just like the final scene of *The Wizard of Oz*, where Dorothy tearfully kisses the Scarecrow, the Tin Man, and the Cowardly Lion before jumping into the hot-air balloon. Dorothy's not the only one. Peter Pan flies back to Neverland, Mary Poppins is whisked away when the wind changes, and ET's spaceship carries him home to his peaceful planet.

It's easy enough to dismiss the Ascension story as a fairytale or first-century science fiction. After all, Jesus had to go somewhere after he rose from the dead, so the first-century Isaac Asimov said, "I know. Let's beam him up. Sounds cool."

It has the awful whiff of a *deus ex machina* ending, except in reverse. Here the God is cranked up from the stage to disappear in a cloud of glory and live happily ever after. We can almost see the scenery shudder, almost catch a glimpse of the dry-ice machine. It's easy enough to see the similarities of the Ascension to fairy-tales, pantomimes, and science-fiction films, and it's easy to assume that since the fairytales are fiction, the Ascension is also fiction.

But what if it's the other way around? We might think the Ascension story is untrue because we have heard similar stories that we know are fantasy. But if the Ascension actually happened as it was reported, then rather than being make-believe like the other stories, it might make us believe the other stories. When something really happens, it makes the fictional accounts truer than they ever were before. Think, for example, of all the fantasy stories about lovelorn princesses marrying handsome princes despite the odds. Then when a real girl finds true love and marries the man of her dreams, does she not make all the fantasy stories come true? When the man is transformed by her radiant and faithful love from a disgusting beast into a reasonably civilized husband and father, have the couple not made all the "Beauty and the Beast" stories come true?

In a similar way, when Someone really does, in a unique incident, ascend into Heaven, he validates all the ancient stories where the hero rises up and flies away home. So, rather than the fantasy stories' making the Gospel story untrue, the Gospel story makes the fantasy stories true in a way they never were before. They become prophecies or a mysterious cultural foreshadowing of an event that really will happen. But for this to be the case, we have to imagine in what way such a seeming fairytale might actually have happened.

Can we even begin to believe that Jesus Christ was beamed up into Heaven? Can we really be serious in imagining that Jesus floated up into the air and disappeared from sight? Why not?

Up, Up, and Away

Levitation is well documented in the annals of mystical phenomena. In fact, it's one of the more common and most reliably witnessed of the supernatural phenomena. Lots of people saw St. Teresa of Avila levitate, and St. Joseph Cupertino was so adept at levitation that he was eventually named patron saint of pilots and airline hostesses.

Levitation isn't even considered very impressive among those who believe. When St. Thomas Aquinas was summoned to witness the remarkable case of a nun floating up to the ceiling, he simply looked up and remarked, "I didn't know nuns wore such big boots." Mystics of other religions have also been observed to defy the normal laws of gravity: fakirs float, gurus hover, poltergeists make heavy objects fly through the air, and the demon-possessed are known both to roar and to soar.

I point this out, not to say that the Ascension was simply a case of anti-gravity technology, teleportation, or levitation, but to make us think again. Maybe reality is rubbery. Strange things happen, and when they do, it's much more natural to exclaim with wonder and curiosity than to deny that such things happen. It's also more fun. When St. Thomas Aquinas saw the levitating nun, he also saw the joke, and that's one of the delightful things about levitation stories. The Ascension is much more important than a simple case of levitation, but the same sense of *joie de vivre* is there, and the Ascension, like levitation, reminds us that the law of gravity is sometimes broken by levity.

If gravity is sometimes defied in a supernatural way, how might this make us reconsider the Ascension of Jesus Christ? The account given in the New Testament says he floated up into the clouds and eventually faded from sight.[42] This is more than levitation. He didn't just go up and come down. He went up, and he disappeared. The story makes it sound as if Jesus, having finished his job on earth, shed his earthly clothes and became less physical. In other words, he turned into a spirit; he was vaporized.

But what if it's the other way around? What if Jesus became, not less physical, but more physical? What if he disappeared because he eventually went into a realm that is not less real, but more real?

How can this be? Am I simply spinning theories and being fanciful? No. I'm serious, and as usual, everything depends on our starting point of view. We naturally assume that this physical world is the real, solid, and substantial realm, while the spiritual realm is ethereal, wispy, transparent, and therefore less real. But who's to say which realm is more real? Most people think the world of spirits is ethereal, while the physical world is solid; but what if it's exactly the other way around? Let's imagine that Aunt Susan said she saw an angel pass through a brick wall. We would assume that the angel was ethereal and "unreal" because we assume the brick wall is solid. But what if angels are more solid than brick walls? If they are, then suddenly it's the brick wall that is ethereal and insubstantial.

How do we know which one passed through the other? Physicists tell us that what we consider solid matter is mostly emptiness and energy. What if the angels (whom we think of as creatures of air and energy) are, in fact, made of something more dense and solid than brick walls? What I mean to say is that an angel's purely spiritual existence might actually be more "solid" than physical matter in our world. If this were so, the angel may have passed through the brick wall as a man passes through a bank of fog. Think about it for a moment. If you didn't know which was more solid — fog or a human being — and you witnessed a man step through a bank of fog wouldn't it be easy to believe that he was ethereal and the fog solid?

Up, Up, and Away

To return to the story of the Ascension, it could be that, while the disciples saw Jesus vaporize into the spiritual realm, in fact he passed through a "cloud of fog" into a realm more solid than this one; from Christ's point of view, he was becoming part of a world far more colorful, vibrant, and alive. What if all the lurid religious art with its ghastly heightened colors and vivid detail points to some reality we hadn't counted on? What if Heaven is as bright, colorful, and flamboyant as a Mardi Gras parade, a fun fair, or a Hindu festival? If this is so, then when Jesus went from this world to the next, he was simply leaving a monochrome world to step into a world of color, where the water is as hard as glass, the light is like crystal, and each grain of dust is as hard and beautiful as a diamond.

You might ask, "Why didn't Jesus just disappear? Why did we have to have this fantastic flight back to Heaven?" I can think of two reasons. The first is a practical one. He couldn't stay around forever on this earth, but if Jesus had just disappeared, everyone would have wondered where he had gotten to. They needed resolution. They needed to see him leave. The second reason is more interesting. They not only needed to see him leave, but they needed to see him leave physically. His Incarnation was real and physical; his death was real and physical; his Resurrection was real and physical; so his Ascension had to be real and physical, too. Furthermore, this real and physical presence had to be taken up into Heaven. Jesus couldn't simply turn into a ghost and flit away, or people might have thought he had been nothing more than a ghost the whole time.

The reason Jesus went up physically has to do with the relationship between our bodies and souls. Humans are physical/spiritual beings. Physicality is an intrinsic part of our spiritual nature. Our bodies aren't shells for our souls; they are integrally linked with our souls. Therefore, when human beings enter the spiritual realm, they must bring their bodies with them, or else end up less than human. They don't become spirits or ghosts; instead their physical-ness becomes spiritualized. Their physical-ness isn't done away with; it's transformed to a higher plane of material reality. If this is so, then the Ascension shows this very process happening. Jesus didn't just become a disembodied spirit. He didn't turn into a ghost; he became a spiritualized physical being, and that's why he couldn't just disappear in a puff of smoke. Instead his body had to be taken up into Heaven.

When Jesus was taken up into Heaven, what really happened was that the door swung open for physical humanity to be divinized. By this action, human flesh entered Heaven; a physical dimension was introduced to the spiritual realm. That is why St. Paul insists that (despite the seeming absurdities) when we die and are resurrected, we shall have what he calls a "resurrection body." The actual physical components won't be reconstituted from dust and ash, but the physical dimension to our nature will live on.

It's difficult to imagine this without imagining that we shall be like ghosts. Turn that on its head by imagining that what we are now is ghostly compared with what we shall be. Those resurrection bodies we are promised will be more real, more youthful, more eternal, and more beautiful than we can ever imagine, and they'll be so much more real than our current bodies that they'll be to these bodies as a real landscape is to a black-and-white photograph of the scene.

Do we have trouble imagining such things? I don't know why. We accept the miracles of technology every day, but if someone had told our grandparents that we could feed a piece of paper into a machine in Peru which would then turn it into a series of bleeps and transmit them thousands of miles to a little machine spinning in space, only to bounce back to another machine in Pennsylvania, which then printed the image onto another piece of paper, they would think we were dangerously mad. If we told our grandparents that a machine the size of a breadbox would transmit the text of a book from California to Karachi in the time it takes you to blink, they would ridicule such fantasies.

So why can we not imagine that similarly unbelievable things might be possible in that last frontier — the one between the physical and the spiritual realms? The person of faith stands on the edge of these possibilities and has room to muse, room to surmise, and room to theorize. After all, with God anything is possible, and it's up to our imagination to try to visualize what it all means, and what kind of world is on the other side. If this is really the last frontier, then suddenly the person of faith isn't an antique leftover of a bygone age, but the dreamer on the cutting edge. Suddenly it's the Man from Missouri with his dull doubt who seems like the antiquarian.

The Ascension simply tells me that the world is open-ended, and that I can expect the unexpected. Furthermore, it tells me that it might happen to me. I can be transformed; I can have commerce with the spiritual world. Do we think that these physical bodies give us pleasure? We haven't yet experienced pleasure. What pleasures we've had here are merely a glimpse or taste of the greater reality that is to come. When you begin to catch a glimpse of this other country, the ancient words ring true, and the heart lifts to think that it really may be so that eye has not seen, nor ear heard, nor the heart of man conceived of such glories that await us.[43]

Chapter Twelve

Ambitiously Ambidextrous

. . . and is seated at the right hand of God, the Father Almighty.

Some time ago I heard a professional theologian being quizzed on the radio about a book he had just written about God. The interviewer was doing his best to trivialize the topic in order to appeal to his audience and to reinforce their secular mind set. He chided the theologian for being credulous. How could he possibly believe in such an outmoded and superstitious thing as the Christian Creed? How could an intelligent modern intellectual believe in such fairytale stuff as angels, miracles, and Jesus sitting on a throne at God's right hand in glory? How could he be so literal?

The theologian politely replied that he didn't really believe God had a right hand or that Jesus sat on a throne in the sky. This was, he explained, a turn of phrase to express the spiritual truth that Jesus was given a place of spiritual power. If he had been given more time, the theologian would have gone on to explain that God is pure spirit. He has no body. He is the Divine Essence, the Supreme Intelligence, the Uncaused Cause, and the Being Beyond all Being. God is the Unimaginable One. In fact, God is so completely beyond human imagination that as soon as we say something about God, we must turn around and say that what we have said is not completely true.

This way of knowing by not knowing is called the *apophatic way*. This particular theologian explained it better than most of his breed, and I'm sure he's right to tell us that God is pure spirit and beyond all our knowing. But when we say, "Everything we think about God is not true," we should be prepared to say that what we have just said is also not true. God is bigger than what we can think, not smaller. We must admit that God is greater than anything we can think or say about him, but when we become too pessimistic about what we can say about God, he very soon turns out to be less than we've said, not more. In other words, if we say nothing about him, he soon turns out to be nothing, and instead of gazing on the Great Presence, we find ourselves staring at a great absence.

Eventually I began to take the side of the terrier-like radio man. I wished he had challenged the theologian a bit more and not allowed him to duck for cover into the nearest metaphor. It sounds good to say, "God doesn't have a right hand and Jesus doesn't sit on a throne in Heaven," but how do we know Jesus doesn't sit on a throne and that God doesn't have a right hand? If Heaven is brighter and bolder, more tangible and physical than we thought, maybe God is, too.

God must be substantial in some way, for is it conceivable that an insubstantial being should have created concrete things? Could a void create a solid? Can something come from nothing? It's true that he is pure spirit, but that spirit has a form appropriate to itself; and if God is the most real of all realities, then that form must be more substantial and "solid" than we can imagine.

Indeed, if God really did take human flesh in Jesus Christ, and if that flesh was brought back to life and taken up into Heaven, then there is a physical dimension united with the Being of God. This is where the phrase "seated at the right hand of the Father" starts to get interesting. The story of the Ascension indicates that Jesus went up into Heaven in bodily form. His body did not disintegrate or disappear, but was somehow transposed into a new dimension of reality. By this action, he must have done something stupendous: he must have integrated, not only the human spiritual nature in the Being of God, but human physical-ness as well. In other words, the human being Jesus Christ is not only the image of God here on earth, but the image of God in Heaven as well: the physical image of man in God, existing like a dynamic, yet static icon at the heart of the Godhead.

If there is a physical dimension to God, it can't be a physical condition as we know it, for part of our physical condition is change and decay. So there must be some way in which God is material and in motion, and yet unchanging. This is what Christians are hinting at when they speak of the Trinity being a unity of dynamic love. In God three Persons exist in one unified nature. The Three are in a constant dance of dynamic interaction while They are also in perfect harmony. This threefold unity spins like a top — in perfect motion, yet perfectly at rest. It's like a mighty waterfall: always in motion, always the same, and never the same. Because the three Persons are in a constant action among themselves, the "physical" aspect of God which Jesus brought with him into Heaven remains real, vital, and eternal.

Another way of thinking of this is that the Son not only sits at the right hand of the Father, but that he is the right hand of the Father. At one point, Jesus himself said that what he did was by the "finger of God."[44] So if he is the finger, he might just as well be the right hand, and if he is the right hand of the Father, then the third person of the Trinity — the Holy Spirit — could be the left hand, making God ambitiously ambidextrous. As a result, the Father clapping his hands with joy and delight at creation might be one of the best images of the Trinity we can come up with. Likewise, when the children sing, "He's got the whole world in his hands," they might be singing the glories of the greatest mystery of them all — the mystery of the most holy, glorious, and undivided Trinity.

So perhaps the doctrine of the Trinity reveals a God in whom the physical and the spiritual exist in an endlessly intricate and fascinating relationship. We sense this dynamic on earth as well. Don't I know myself to be most physical and most spiritual when I'm in a relationship with someone? On my own, I may descend to a state of simple brutish physicality and extinguish the spirit, or I may pursue a twisted solitary and ascetic life, becoming so "spiritual" that I quench the physical altogether. However, when I'm making love or punching someone in the nose or laughing at a joke or listening to a bore or sharing a pint of beer with a friend, I'm most alive as a human being. And that means I'm most fully and unself-consciously alive in both a physical and spiritual way at the same time.

This is why people get married, join a club, play football, go to the theater, and join a church: so they can be in a relationship with others that's both spiritual and physical. When they do, they know they're more alive than they can be in any other way. Whenever we get together in a relationship, there's a physical and a spiritual element at work — even if in a degraded and degrading manner. But when Christians go to church, the two elements of the physical and spiritual are brought together explicitly. At church they do something spiritual through a physical action: they join the body of Christ by getting dunked into a tank of water. They renew their membership by eating bread and drinking wine — which have themselves been transformed into something that's a supernatural union of the physical and spiritual.

Finally, if the truth that Jesus Christ is "seated at the right hand of the Father" indicates that somehow the physical is a part even of God himself, then suddenly the physical is important. More than ever, matter matters. If this is so, then what I do with this physical life of mine may turn out to be just as important as what I do with my spiritual life. If the two are intertwined, they affect each other. This has been part of Christian teaching since time immemorial. With this body I may turn my soul toward Hell, or with this body I may turn my soul toward Heaven. If this is the case, then the little physical things are important, and that is why Christ said God has numbered the hairs of our head and knows when a sparrow falls, and that we will be judged for every idle word spoken.[45] In other words, because Jesus is seated at God's right hand, every little decision, word, and action matters. If the little actions matter, then I may turn toward the outer darkness with something as small as sneering at my neighbor, or I may start the long journey home with an action as small as getting down on my knees.

Chapter Thirteen

Myths, Movies, and Medieval Cathedrals

He will come again to judge the living and the dead.

I like movies. I don't go in for those sophisticated French films in which men and women smoke cigarettes in bed and discuss the meaning of life in anguished whispers. Neither am I a fan of serious films with social messages. No, I like *Hollywood* pictures: big heroes, big villains, and big explosions. I'm a sucker for an engaging plot and a happy ending. And in almost every popular movie, the bad guy loses and the good guy wins.

The cynic will observe that this is because the marketing men have figured out that audiences like happy endings. This is probably true, but what interests me is why the crowds like happy endings, and what kind of happy endings they like. They don't like happy endings per se, because they don't want a happy ending for everyone. They only want the good people to be happy. They want the bad people to be unhappy at the end.

In fact, the ordinary person doesn't like happy endings; he likes endings that are just. That's why ordinary people also enjoy a tragedy, because in a classical tragedy, a flawed hero gets what's coming to him, and what's coming is not a happy ending.

People have demanded that their drama end with justice ever since the first storyteller sat down beside the campfire. The search for meaning, and therefore for justice, has always been at the heart of storytelling. Through their stories, ordinary people worked out the rules and guidelines of justice. They told others how to live and what payment to expect for their pains as well as for their pleasures. The gods and goddesses — whether they live on Mount Olympus or in Beverly Hills — remind ordinary people about good and evil and the final reward.

People have a universal sense that right and wrong exist, and that it's right to punish evil and reward goodness. But our perspective on justice is limited. The justice we desire isn't always the justice we deserve. Justice is possible only when we have all the facts, and because of our limited understanding, it's impossible for us to judge perfectly. Judgment Day is bound to hold surprises for everyone.

This element of surprise was impressed upon me about fifteen years ago, when I visited the magnificent Cathedral of Chartres in France. Living in that city at the time was an eccentric Englishman who had dedicated his life to giving English-speaking tours of the cathedral, and I happened to find myself on one of his famous excursions. Toward the end of our tramp around this most awesome temple to the Incarnation of the Son of God, we wound up at the great South Door. Over the portal is a carving of the Last Judgment, with Christ seated on the judgment throne. Before him stands St. Michael with his scales of justice. On the righthand side, graves are being opened, and angels are assisting the righteous to rise up to eternal life. On the left, grimacing demons spear the wicked and push them down into the everlasting fires.

Then the Englishman pointed out a detail that caught my attention. "Look at the souls coming out of their graves," he said.

"Notice how the stone-carver seven hundred years ago took the trouble to carve the faces on both the damned and the saved with an expression of surprise." When I looked closely, I saw he was right. People on both sides registered surprise at the outcome. This in itself is a surprising observation. It's also a sensible observation because those who are destined for Heaven are humble, so they'll be surprised because they don't think they deserve Heaven. At the same time, those who are damned, being proud, are sure they don't deserve Hell. The further surprise was that among the damned were a couple of bishops and monks, while among the saved were women and men who, by their dress, had clearly lived for pleasure.

Making the judgment a surprise is the kind of subversion that's totally consistent with the Gospel stories. Jesus constantly told stories about death and judgment that turned things upside down, upset everyone's complacency, and made them think again. The One who turned over the tables in the Temple turned over everyone's expectations. At the final judgment, he will turn them over again. If true justice considers and weighs up all the facts, it must happen, as my English friend observed, at the end of time. Since this is so, there is naturally an awful lot of room for surprise.

Consider the nameless stone-carver at Chartres seven hundred years ago. Carving those faces was perhaps just another day's work. He did his best and was intelligent enough to understand why the faces should show surprise. He probably died as he lived — as a poor, unknown craftsman. Then one day hundreds of years later, an eccentric tour guide notices the detail and passes it on to thousands of pilgrims. I hear the story and tell many people, and now you are reading it in this book. Perhaps you'll be inspired and one day go out to change the world with a life on fire with goodness and love. And that humble stone-carver in France so long ago will get some of the credit.

This is the surprising nature of Providence, and why studying the ways of God's will in the world is far more interesting than the most intricately woven plot of any drama, movie, or novel. The tiniest seeds may grow into the greatest of trees; the tiniest action may bring about the greatest result. Who at the time would have imagined, for instance, that the political execution of a small-town street preacher would redeem the world? This everlasting plot twist is one of the most fascinating and absorbing aspects of the Last Judgment.

In one sense, the death of this preacher is the Last Judgment itself.

Christians spend time contemplating the Cross because in that action at the center point of time, they see that somehow, through the death of this preacher, Judgment Day has already come. We said the Judgment Day would be surprising. This is not only surprising, but shocking, for there where mercy was denied, mercy is given. There where justice was denied, justice is given. As the man who incarnates God, Jesus Christ is able to pronounce the judgment, and as the man who encapsulates humanity, he is able to absorb the punishment. Thus, on the Cross, judgment and mercy are fused in one action. There the God-Man becomes the judge and the judged, the priest and the victim, the executioner and the executed. There in an economical and shocking transaction, God neatly turns the tables and allows the final judgment to take another turn. As the plot turns, the agenda of the judgment is suddenly transformed. It's changed because the price has been paid. Forgiveness is possible because the crucified Christ, with his arms outstretched, offers justice from one hand and mercy from the other.

Suddenly the judgment isn't simply a weighing of our good and evil deeds, but our response to this moment of judgment and mercy that has already happened. Let's face it: if the judgment were based simply on the balance of our good or evil deeds, there would be little room for real surprise, because we would all be headed down, not up. But once the possibility of forgiveness is thrown into the bargain, the end of the story isn't decided. There is room for choice, and once there is choice, there is room for surprise.

There are those who deny the judgment; but if anything is true, the judgment must be true. What I mean is that, for there to be such a thing as truth at all, there must logically be such a thing as judgment, because judgment is simply the final proclamation and clear resolution of truth. As St. Paul put it, "Now we see as through a glass darkly. Then we shall see him face-to-face."[46] In other words, the time must come when all falsehood fades away; all dissimulation, phoniness, and presumption are revealed to be a cheap charade. Then the truth shall be told. All shall be revealed. What is secret shall be shouted from the housetops.[47] Truth is something that has an inner, inexorable drive to be revealed. It can't be concealed forever. Like Dostoevsky's murderer in *Crime and Punishment,* the grisly story can't be suppressed. Truth will out.

If truth, like light, can't finally be hidden, then lies, on the other hand, have a built-in instability. They have a natural inclination to disintegrate, topple, and fall. As a result, there must come a time — if not in this life, then in the next — when all the paper pride, tinselly show, and shallow trickery of deceit and self-deceit must be stripped away. Judgment Day is that time. For the medieval stone-carver, this included Christ on his judgment seat, weighing up the good and evil we have done or not done, and this image is as good as any. After all, Jesus Christ claimed to be the Truth as well as the Way and the Life. Seeing him as he really is will be the very essence of judgment. In fact, why do we need anything else? To see him will be to reveal our whole lives for what they really were. In his light, we shall see light.[48] In his light, we shall also see darkness, perhaps for the first time; and for most people a true vision of both the horror of the dark and the glory of the light will be judgment itself.

At that point, all the choices we will have made will be summarized by one choice. That choice is our response to the judgment that has already been given.

The judgment pronounced is the undebatable verdict of "guilty" and the unexpected offer of clemency: you may be forgiven if you will. At that point, every knee shall bow and every tongue confess that Jesus Christ is Lord.[49] After their initial surprise, some will confess his Lordship through gritted teeth, bowing the knee with terror in their hearts until the very end. They will reject the mercy with fury. To see him will be to see everything they have always hated and despised. To see him will be to acknowledge that they were wrong, very wrong about everything, and at that point, even the good things they will have done will be soured by their rebellion and become for them the desperate decisions of the damned. Then the worst surprise will be that they were surprised at all, for their whole lives will then have been revealed to be one long, sordid decision to turn away from God to serve only themselves.

For others, in seeing him they will see the Beauty they have always adored, the Truth they have always sought, and the Mercy they always hoped existed. Even those who unknowingly have followed the light will be taken into the light. At that point, all their decisions and deeds will be redeemed. They will be surprised because for them nothing was wasted. Everything was gathered up, and even the sordid deeds and decisions will have been turned around. Their decisions and deeds, which were spotted with shadow, will be revealed as dappled glories. Their wrong turnings will prove to have been the scenic route, their failures learning points, their battle scars red badges of courage. After the initial surprise, they, too, will wonder why they were surprised at all, for the judgment was simply the summary and fulfillment of their whole lifelong search for their Master.

Because the judgment can't come until the end of time, and because it will be full of surprises, we're told not to attempt eternal judgments in this life. We can and must make moral judgments about acts, but how can we ever analyze the mass of hidden motives in a person's soul? How can we negotiate the labyrinth of our own hidden desires, our unconscious instincts, and the circumstances of our crimes? Only God has the eternal perspective and omniscient insight needed to pull that off.

Better simply to trust and obey. Better to throw ourselves on the mercy. Better to trust the Judge who knows all, since to know all is to forgive all. In the meantime, if we take such a view, we can live in freedom. As the greatest modern saint teaches us, we can simply trust in God like little children. We can live each day to the best of our ability and have no thought for tomorrow. We can look to the flowers of the field and the birds of the air and learn from them how to live. They do not toil; they do not spin.[50] They do not judge. If we can only cultivate that kind of simple trust, then, when the end comes, we might just awaken from our sleep with a gasp of surprise and find ourselves being lifted up to a burning justice that has already been completed by mercy.

Chapter Fourteen

Nature's Bonfire, World's Wildfire

I believe in the Holy Spirit . . .

When they took a census in England a few years ago, there was a whimsical religious revolution led by *Star Wars* fans. They encouraged people to write "Jedi" in the "Religion" space on their census form. I had heard only a few months before about one British *Star Wars* fan who watches the film every Sunday morning. (I knew *Star Wars* was a cult movie, but I didn't know it had actually become a cult.) This is the sort of gesture I find entertaining, and I resisted putting "Jedi" on my own form only out of a conviction that the Christians needed all the help they could get.

One has to look on the bright side. This might be the start of an exciting trend. It may be the way to get people back to church. Disenchanted clergymen looking for a new idea could install wide screens in their churches and beckon more of the *Star Wars* faithful to participate in the cosmic clash between good and evil each Sunday. With a bit of musical ingenuity, the *Star Wars* theme music could be developed into a very stirring processional hymn. Acolytes could be dressed in Obi-Wan Kenobi robes and carry light sabers instead of candles. The Liturgy could begin with, "The

Force be with you." To which all reply, "And also with you." For special music, Han could sing a solo.

The Jedi religion is a spoof, but truth is spoken in jest; and the fact that a science-fiction spoof-religion exists is a clear indication of the famine of real religion and myth in our culture. We shouldn't complain too much. The truth is that the *Star Wars* films may be the only religion or theology many people get. The films might just remind the audience that there is a battle between good and evil going on, and that there are actually people who dedicate their lives to a courageous and mystical pursuit of honor, valor, and peace. The movies keep alive the rumor that there is a force that is with you, and that this supernatural force is not only real, but really believed in by millions of ordinary people.

Obi-Wan Kenobi's "Force" is the same power of which the poets sing. It's the Spirit of Beauty, the "force that through the green fuse drives the flower." It's the "dearest freshness deep down things," "unknown modes of Being,"[51] and the "awful shadow of some unseen Power."[52] It's "a motion and a spirit, that impels all thinking things, all objects of thought and rolls through all things."[53] The philosopher Heraclitus thought this essential life force was best symbolized by fire. In fact, when asked what essence the world was made of, Heraclitus, who lived six centuries before the Christians, foreshadowed their doxology with the words, "This world . . . was ever, is now, and ever shall be an everlasting Fire."

The fact that fire might represent the force of nature is easy enough to understand. Indeed, fire is an excellent symbol for the life force, because it's the most vivid and primeval energy source known to man. It's an energy source that is both terrifying and comforting, mysterious and practical. One can understand the reasonableness of the symbol, but what interests me is the rationale for it. Heraclitus chose fire because he was trying to explain how nature could be both one and many at the same time. In other words, how can there be an essential unity when there are so many individual entities? How can there be one unifying force while there are a multitude of individual living things? How can there be a single power while there are also many beings that exercise power?

Heraclitus concluded that there had to be an eternal essence that was itself unified and unchanging, but which enabled individual changing things to exist. Fire provided the perfect symbol for the philosopher, because fire is constantly the same, yet it assumes many constantly changing forms. His "fire force" is also a unifying force. For Heraclitus, fire symbolizes an energy source that runs like a current of electricity through all living things, and thereby links them together.

The fact that a Greek philosopher six centuries before Christ saw fire as the essential force tickles my imagination, because fire is the primary symbol Christians use for the Holy Spirit. Some people put down Christianity because it seems to have stolen beliefs and ideas from other religions. So the critics, knowing that Heraclitus thought the driving force of nature was fire, and seeing that the Christian Holy Spirit is also symbolized by fire, blame the Christians for pinching a good idea.

But Heraclitus wasn't the only one to think of using fire as a symbol for the Essential Energy. The eternal flame burns in the temples of most religions, and fire burns throughout the ancient Hebrew stories in many forms. An angel with a fiery sword expels Adam and Eve from Eden. A fire burns on the altar as Abraham almost sacrifices his son. God speaks to Moses from a bush that burns but isn't consumed. The Jews are led from Egypt by a fiery pillar and establish a temple where lamps and altar fires burn perpetually to mark the presence of their God.

But even if someone did borrow a previously existing religious idea, there's nothing wrong with that. All the greatest artists admit that their best ideas are stolen. What's important isn't whether you steal an idea, but what you do with it. What Christians did wasn't so much a case of stealing a treasure as picking up a football that has been fumbled and running with it. With their theology of the Holy Spirit, Christians picked up a universal, but vague, religious symbol and made it far more sophisticated, precise, and revolutionary. They took the symbol and connected it to the reality to which it pointed. They particularized what had been universal and specified what had been vague. They looked past the shadowy force and saw the person who had cast the shadow.

The reasoning goes like this: Within nature there seems to be a life force that guides, directs, and empowers growth. We can also suppose that this power inspires ideas and sparks change in the world. It's pleasant to think of this "force" as a sort of random energy system empowering all living things. But if we think about this vague force for very long, we realize that it is not just a random, chthonic energy field. It does particular things. It behaves in a characteristic way. Soon we are talking about "a motion and a spirit, that impels all thinking things, all objects of thought and rolls through all things."

Could a force that impels thinking things *not* be a thinking thing itself? Is it simply what electricity is to a computer, or is it more like what the programmer is to the computer?

It's both. It empowers, but it empowers with purpose. If it's a single force, then it's unified. Because it's unified, it must be integrated with itself and with all physical things. If this is true, then this power must be a force for unity and harmony, not for chaos and fragmentation. If it's a force for unity, then mustn't it have a particular purpose? If it has a purpose, it must have a will, and if it has a will, mustn't it be a person? This is why the Christian thinkers pondered over the teachings they had received using the philosophical tools of the age, and concluded that the Holy Spirit wasn't a blind force, but a person, the "third Person of the Trinity." He might seem vague and shadowy, but that's only because He's shy. He's not the main actor out on stage. He's one of those geniuses behind the scenes.

When you recognize that this "force of nature" is in fact a person, with a distinct character, the whole world becomes more personal. It's part of our culture to regard nature as a vast machine or an intricate and cold computer. But the sophisticated ancients saw nature, not as a complex computer, but as a complex community. They didn't perceive nature as a cold and calculating formula, but as a warm and whimsical family. For them the sun was a father, the moon a mother. The sea was a terrible, grumpy uncle, and the planets were distant cousins. For them the forests surged with the familiar spirits of the trees and the streams. There were personalities for almost everything, from the planets and the stars to the pebbles and the starfish. Indeed, the whole of the unseen world was thronged with half creatures — angels and demons, gods and goddesses, mythical beasts and magical creatures.

This kind of joyful and terrible paganism isn't Christian, but it's closer to Christianity than the current mind set that treats the created order (including human beings) as nothing more than chemical machines. To illustrate the point: no one thought it heretical for St. Francis to call the Sun his brother and the Moon his sister, or for him to call the running streams and burning fires his brothers and sisters. Francis, like the pagans, sensed the personal nature of Nature. But unlike the pagans, he realized that the pretty poetry of fairies, dryads, and naiads was pointing to a greater power. Because he was a Christian, Francis realized that all the lesser personalities were subject to one great Person. If you like, Francis called the Sun his brother because the Son of God was his brother, and he sang a hymn to the fire "masterful and bright" because the Fire of the Holy Spirit had become his bright master.

This brings us back to Heraclitus, because his symbol of fire is the unifying force that brings together the one and the many. In Christian terms, the fire force of the Holy Spirit links the one power behind and above all things with the power that is within and through all things. In other words, the Holy Spirit is without and within, immanent and transcendent, driving all things in the created order, and yet above and beyond them. This Holy Spirit isn't just a force of creation. It's a creative person. Furthermore, like all creative spirits, the Holy Spirit never rests. He is constantly surging with fresh ideas, new initiatives, and sparks of sudden fire. The aim of this creative force is to bring the whole crumbling and chaotic creation back into order, harmony, and unity.

The Holy Spirit does this through people. That is always the way to change anything. You may have five-year plans, expensive campaign strategies, and extensive goals for achievement, but for any change to happen, particular actions have to be taken by particular people. The individual who effected this reconciliation of all that was fragmented and chaotic was the one who was most empowered by the Holy Spirit: Jesus Christ. In fact, he was so filled with the Holy Spirit that he was one with that Spirit. Part of the plan for his life was that he was to plant the seed of that Spirit within the human race. By planting the seed of his body in the earth by dying, the Holy Spirit was released to raise a crop of a new kind of humanity.

This new breed of person was to have a share of Christ's own Spirit. The one Spirit surging through creation was to become specified in individual people. That's why Moses could see a burning bush only outside himself, but at Pentecost Peter had the burning fire first alight on his head, then burn its way into his heart, his mind, and every fiber of his being. He was zapped, if you like, by the Heraclitean fire. This spiritual immolation effected a total transformation in his life. He went from being a cowardly liar who betrayed his best friend to a man who by his fearlessness would change the course of history.

The first Christians who experienced this stunning transformation believed not only that Jesus Christ was still alive, but that he was alive in them. They said they were brought into union with Christ. This wasn't simply the unity that football players or members of an orchestra or a club might experience with one another. When the first Christians said they were united with Christ, they meant that they were drawn into a kind of marriage with him: two persons permeating and interpenetrating each other, united in a bond that is physical, mental, and spiritual.

Stand on your head, and take a fresh look at the implications of this. We're not talking about a religion that simply puts people in touch with a benevolent force that will help them through life. We're not promoting a religion that just helps people to be good or to make the world a better place. We're not even offering a spirit guide that helps people to be as much like Jesus Christ as possible. It's not just about saying prayers and being good. This is about being remade into radiant beings who exist in a dynamic union with God.

The New Testament says that, by the action of the Spirit, we have become God's adopted sons and daughters.[54] Christ was God's Son, so, by the work of the Holy Spirit, we're being transformed into little Christs, and we become "sons in the Son."

This isn't a religion that makes people good, but a religion that makes people gods.

The first Christian theologians recognized this and called the process "divinization." They actually said, "In Christ, God became man so that men could become gods." A memorial to this truth exists in the center of Rome. There you'll find the ancient temple called the Pantheon. It was built to honor all the ancient gods, but when the Christians took it over, they named it the Church of All Saints because in the new religion, it was ordinary men and women, transformed by the Holy Spirit, who supplanted the old gods and goddesses to become the new hosts of Heaven.

If this is what Christianity is really about, then what a shallow farce we have made of it all when we reduce the whole thing to a set of rules for respectable behavior, or to a social club, or to a charity. No wonder no one wants to be a Christian if the whole thing is no more than etiquette for social climbers! Similarly, if the work of the Holy Spirit is divinization, how puerile to reduce the whole matter to a flurry of religious emotion featuring specious miracles, waving hands, and bottoms waggling to the beat of sentimental music. If the whole business is about spousal unity with the God of stupendous power and radiant goodness, then how ridiculous to turn the church into a political pressure group, a theology shop, or a group-therapy session.

The goal of this individual transformation is to be united with the One who created the whole universe to start with, and this brings us back to the reconciliation of the one and the many that Heraclitus dreamed about, but could never imagine.

However, to say that we're united with God isn't to suggest that we're simply absorbed into him — as a minnow might be swallowed by a whale, or a raindrop by the ocean. Our individuality isn't annihilated by this process: it's fulfilled. Instead of being absorbed, we're adopted. We're given our proper place in the hierarchy of being.

We take our place in a great dance. We step out in time to the same rhythm to which the stars, all the whirling planets, and the whole order of creation moves in measured beauty. Our final destiny is a homecoming, a wedding reception, a celebration meal, or a family feast. Our final destiny is to be united as a reconciled child is united with his family when he takes his proper place at the table.

This kind of reconciliation brings us into unity with him, but it also brings us into unity with ourselves, with all those who are our brothers and sisters in faith, and with the whole created order. This is why, when the Holy Spirit rushed down with such touching enthusiasm at Pentecost, he not only transformed the lives of individuals, but he established an unbreakable link between them all. The Holy Spirit runs through all Christians like an electric and energetic bloodline, binding them all together. This is why that same event is considered the Church's birthday, because the Church is that amazing and awesome institution that gathers together in a mystical bond all those who have received the same Holy Spirit.

Here on earth the Church is a fractured image of the final unity to which humanity is called. Like a jigsaw puzzle that hasn't yet been completed, the picture of our final reconciliation is discernible, but still broken. That broken picture exists wherever two or three gather to keep the flame alive. Believe it or not, that local congregation of ordinary people who sing out of tune and fight with one another over who will arrange the flowers is a microcosm of the eternal ranks of saints and angels who circle day and night around the throne of God. There in the pews, that gathering of beautiful saints and horrific sinners is a pointer to that final collection of humanity, whose depth, breadth, beauty, and mystery can't be imagined. For in each of those flawed and frail human beings, the fire of creation burns, and will burn, until by a final purgation they're transformed into all they were created to be.

Chapter Fifteen

The Universal Corner Shop

. . . the holy Catholic Church . . .

One of the delightful things about converting to the Catholic Church is that it's shocking. If you want to be a nonconformist, upset people's expectations, and be genuinely subversive, become a Catholic. Mention the name of almost any other religion, and you will probably evoke a yawn. Say "holy Catholic Church," and you're bound to get a strong response, and most often that response is negative. Since Jesus Christ said, "Woe to you when all men speak well of you,"[55] it would seem that the Catholic Church is particularly blessed.

One of the most powerful hints that her claims are authentic is that the Catholic Church is barely tolerated and often attacked by nearly everyone who is outside the Church. (That is exactly what Jesus told his followers to expect; so when a particular church is regularly vilified, this is a clue that it's more authentic.) It's true that adversity makes strange bedfellows, and there's no bed more full of opposites than the anti-Catholic bed. All sorts of Protestants, from suave theologians to snake handlers, are suddenly allies in their attacks on Rome. Antipathy toward the Catholic

Church unites Communists and Ku Klux Klan members, Anglicans and atheists, Eastern Orthodox and Evangelicals, Methodists and Mormons. When faced with the ancient foe of the Roman Church, feminists embrace freemasons, and freedom fighters befriend fascists.

Try a little experiment. Just for fun, if you aren't already Catholic, tell people you've decided to convert. Your friends with taste will tease you for liking plastic snowstorm paperweights with miniature basilicas inside, paintings of Mary on black velvet, and pictures of Jesus with googly eyes. At the same time your friends who pride themselves on being "plain folk" will blame you for a sudden interest in Baroque architecture, lacy vestments, and Monteverdi Masses. Educated colleagues will denounce you for joining an ignorant and unthinking religion that demands blind obedience, while your less-educated friends will think you've been seduced by philosophical mumbo-jumbo. Your populist critic will blame you for being elitist, while the snob will smile sadly and say that you've chosen to mix with peasants, simpletons, and working-class drones. "Spiritual" friends will be incredulous at your acceptance of a rigid, dogmatic, and hierarchical system, while your theologically minded friends will say you've gone in for mysticism and mushy spirituality. Your liberal friends will shake their heads in dismay at the thought that you would submit to an authoritarian and misogynist regime, while your conservative friends won't understand how you can possibly agree with a Church that promotes social-welfare programs, opposes the death penalty, and is in favor of ecology, ecumenism, and interfaith dialogue.

If everyone attacked the Catholic Church for the same huge and terrible crimes — as they do Hitler, Pol Pot, or Bin Laden — we'd have to conclude that the Catholic Church was indeed a most terrible organization, and every good man and true should

rise up against her. But since the attacks are on totally contradictory fronts, don't we have to suspect that there might be a
problem, not with the attacked, but with the attackers?

What is it about the Catholic Church that warrants such dis-
approval? Is there any other organization in the world that's so
commonly misunderstood, mocked, and maligned by people with
opposite opinions?

Isn't there something in this paradox that rings true? Doesn't
the fact that so many people are annoyed by the Catholic Church
make it perversely attractive? Doesn't this weird contradiction
make you want to join? After all, where else can you enjoy the delicious feeling of belonging to a subversive undercover army while
at the same time belonging to the world's most established and
venerable organization? Where else can you belong to an elite
group of initiated members while also affirming your membership
in the whole family of the human race? Only here can you belong
to a ragtag company of sinners on earth while also being part of the
whole company of Heaven.

This contradiction demands an explanation. I think the reason
the Catholic Church disagrees in some way with everybody is because she must agree in all ways with Somebody: her task is to
please God, not man.

The same is true of people with high ideals and ambitious
goals. They'll agree with those who have similarly high ideals, but
disagree with them beyond the point that their ideals diverge. So
if I set out to climb Mount Everest, and begin by boarding a bus in
London, I will share a certain unity of purpose — a certain agree-
ment — with all my fellow travelers heading east, while simultaneously disagreeing with everyone stopping at Dover, Dubai, or
Delhi. I'm going in the same general direction with them all and
may travel quite a long way with someone who's headed for the

Himalayas, but eventually I'll have to part company with every traveler not headed for the top of Everest.

For the Catholic Church, the truth rises up majestically like Everest waiting to be conquered. Like Everest, the mountain called "truth" is an arduous and risky climb. There are many wrong turns on the way and all too many chances to fall over an edge or plunge into a crevasse — and certainly the Catholic Church has stumbled and fallen many times in her ascent. Yet despite all her problems and human failures, she has picked herself up, dusted herself off, and kept on climbing.

One of the things we learn in the climb is that truth is double-edged, like a sword. The reason the Church disagrees with so many is because she is constantly trying to affirm both sides of the truth at once, and of course that is annoying for everyone who can see only one side.

People are often annoyed on an intellectual level by the claims of the holy Catholic Church, but more often their reaction is an emotional one. When people hear the words *holy Catholic Church*, they may imagine the imposing façade of St. Peter's in Rome and a labyrinthine power structure with innumerable sinister men dressed in red and black. Perhaps they have mental pictures of grim-faced nuns in repressive costumes or dour monks thrashing school-children into submission. I'm not denying that all this may be a part of the Catholic experience, but it's a part of the whole Faith just as a chamber of horrors is part of the amusement park. We would be wrong to assume that the spooks in the ghost house are the whole story. Even so, these lurid impressions of the "holy Catholic Church" are mostly emotional reactions to what is essentially a lucid and precise phrase.

To cut through the lurid to find the lucid, look at the words more simply. The first word of this phrase is *holy*. For most people, "holiness" is the same as piety, and that means wide-eyed missionaries, rosary-stroking old ladies, and eager boys with their trousers hitched up, sporting big smiles and bigger Bibles. The problem here is that we've fallen for a counterfeit. As in any question of authenticity, the genuine article often lies hidden. Real holiness is humble, and humble people, by definition, don't draw attention to themselves. In fact, there are huge numbers of genuinely holy people, but they don't stand out. Finding them is like a game of hide-and-seek. Even when you do find a holy person, he'll laugh at you and deny heartily that he is holy. And that is the sign of his authenticity.

There are many radiantly holy people hidden in the Catholic Church, but in this phrase of the Creed, the word *holy* takes on the purer and simpler sense of "whole" or "complete": simple, integrated, and unified. This meaning of *holy* is linked with goodness in a different way. A thing that is holy is good, not because it's moral, and not because it's trying hard to be better than everything else, but because it's simply what it should be — what God ordained it to be. So when we say that the Church is "holy," we're not saying that she is always totally clean and pure and pious and sinless. History corrects that mistake. Instead, we're saying that the Church is whole and complete, unified and integrated. She is what she should be. In other words, her teaching, practice, and worship form an integrated, consistent, and beautiful unity.

Part of this integrated wholeness is the fact that the Church includes both the humble and the hypocritical. The Catholic Church contains the best and worst of humankind. The history of the Catholic Church reads like the Old Testament. It's full of blood and thunder, crammed with real people who enter the great battle and sometimes win and sometimes lose. The winners rise with a radiance and integrity that is overwhelming in its magnitude. But the spectacular losers are also part of the picture, and they also contribute in a tragic way to the Church's authenticity. Doesn't it seem real that there are both sinners and saints in the Church? Wouldn't you be suspicious if everything were totally spotless, squeaky clean, triumphant, and sinless? Isn't that why you dislike those smiling preachers with their perfect teeth, perfect hair, and perfectly big bank accounts? When you see religious perfection of that kind, don't you smell a rat? A church like that isn't holy. It's full of holes. It leaks.

The second word in this phrase is *Catholic*. Before I was a Catholic, I immediately imagined large, dark churches where banks of candles gutter before austere images of dead saints. I imagined corpulent Renaissance popes sending armies out to fight while they told Michelangelo how to paint. I imagined altars and sacrifices, priests in black, prayers with beads, and people going up steps on their knees. There may be a whole range of other impressions that the word *Catholic* summons up, and they may be bright or shadowy images, depending on our own experience. But to cut through all those personal images, the word *catholic* at its simplest level means "universal." In other words, the Church exists and thrives everywhere and at every time since she was founded by Jesus Christ two thousand years ago.

This is another astounding fact about the Catholic Church that's easily overlooked. In an age of multinational companies, the Catholic Church is really the only multinational religion. It's global. The other religions, sects, and cults are confined by all sorts of boundaries. Sometimes they're limited by the theology or politics of their founders and the circumstances in which they lived. So the Protestant Christians are defined and limited by the theological and political events of the sixteenth century. As a result, many Protestants are fighting on battlefields where the enemy has long departed. (For example, they rail heartily against the corrupt papacy — not noticing that the present pope is a magnificent Christian.) The Anglicans and Eastern Orthodox groups are defined and limited by their national history and ethnic culture. Thus, it's both charming and ridiculous to find Anglican Africans using a sixteenth-century prayer book to sing choral Evensong, or to find Americans named Curtis changing their name to Kallistos when they convert to Greek Orthodoxy.

Similarly, Asian religions find it difficult to escape from Asian culture, and Islam struggles to fit into a modern, liberal technocracy. The other world religions have tried to migrate, but so far they have not proved to be very good travelers. Catholicism, on the other hand, has an amazing capacity to adapt and survive. It adopts new ways and adapts to them like a chameleon while never sacrificing the ancient essentials of the Faith. Like a weed, Catholicism can grow anywhere. You may poison it or pull it up, but it keeps coming back.

Of course, simply because other religions don't travel quite so well doesn't mean that they're worthless. Indeed, there's much that's good and true within all religions, and it's important for Catholics to recognize the truth and goodness in all other religions. One of the most paradoxically impressive things about Catholicism is its universal attitude of affirmation. On the one hand, it makes unique and stupendous claims about its own authenticity, while, on the other, it affirms the goodness and truth found in other religions. "If there is truth there," it seems to say, "we will have it. We recognize it. We can make room for it." This confident open-mindedness is another sign of its magnificent universality.

No other religion, sect, or cult dares to make such universal claims as the Catholic Church does. But while the Catholic Church claims to be universal, she is also as local as the corner shop. If you want to find the Catholic Church, you don't have to go to Rome. That's just where the international offices are. The Catholic Church is St. Walburga's or St. Mary Magdalene's around the corner from your house. There the whole universal Catholic Church, majestic and monumental down the ages, is present in a local microcosm. There you'll find Catholics from every social class, every race, and every age group. Other Christian groups gather according to social, economic, and educational divisions. In the Catholic Church, rich and poor, young and old, black and white, professional and unemployed, men and women, liberal and conservative, saints and sinners all gather together in an astounding unity. In what other human grouping of any kind will you find such a vast array of different individuals united around a shared goal?

Down through the ages people have had dreams of one united human family. From the Tower of Babel to the Third Reich, men have been trying to establish a single world system. Whether it's with armies or politics or economics, the underlying goal of human endeavor has been to knit together a pan-global unifying system wherein divisions will cease and mankind can live together in harmony and brotherly love.

But the emperors and economists have missed the point. All the generals and general secretaries, the presidents and prime ministers, haven't picked up on the fact that this universal convocation of humanity already exists. It has existed for two thousand years. It has an integrated work force. It has over a billion loyal members. It has a centralized leadership that instructs, not only the minds, but also the hearts of its members. It binds together the whole human race with shared dreams, shared aspirations, and a common goal of nothing less than the salvation of the world and the reconciliation and unification of all human beings.

That organization is the holy Catholic Church: and while other empires rise and fall, in every age she carries on her mission, despite persecution from without and corruption from within, confident in the promise of her Founder that even the gates of Hell cannot prevail against her.[56]

Chapter Sixteen

Encyclopedic Sanctity

. . . the Communion of Saints . . .

Anyone who visits a Catholic cathedral in Spain will find the
place a surrealistic cross between a religious shrine, a wax-museum
chamber of horrors, and a medieval market. First of all, the place is
likely to be noisy, with chattering people doing everything from
praying and sightseeing to selling postcards. The noise of clucking
poultry may make you wonder whether you've stumbled into the
weekly livestock market, and when you have a look, you may indeed see a cage of chickens suspended from the ceiling.

Wander further, and you'll see a painting of a levitating saint
in ecstasy or a bank of candles guttering in front of a Madonna
dressed in a cloth of gold with a little crown on her head. There
will be flowers, old ladies dressed in black wearing veils, little
boys playing hide-and-seek, and a line of people standing by something that looks like an ornate privy, but which you know is a
confessional.

If you turn the corner into a side chapel, you may find the
arm bone of a saint or a life-size crucifix, complete with every detail of Jesus Christ's suffering. There's a famous one in Burgos that

actually has human hair and glass eyes, and was reputed to be covered with human skin (it turned out to be cowhide).

All of this is horrific to those who prefer their religion (like their lives) to be sensible, clean, and neat. It's also distasteful for those who like their religion to be lofty, sublime, and intellectual. If truth be told, those who prefer aesthetic Christianity really prefer aesthetics to Christianity. Some of us actually like the Mediterranean brand of Christianity. The Spanish cathedral has romance, mystery, hilarious incongruity, cruelty, tenderness, absurdity, and charm. All of life is there. So Spanish Christianity, complete with cowhide crucifixes, children, and chickens is a reminder that in the Creed we say that we believe in the "Communion of Saints."

Normally when people say this phrase, they mean that they're in the same club as all the Christians who have ever been alive in every place and at every time. This is fine, but the word saints can mean not only holy people, but also holy things. In other words, when you say, "I believe in the Communion of Saints," you're saying that you're united, not only with all those alive in God, but with everything everywhere that is good, beautiful, true, and holy.

In the Catholic Faith, this communion with everything that is good, beautiful, true, and holy is a strange reality. The Catholic Faith is vast, and it includes virtually everything that is true — whether it's an attractive truth or a terrible truth — no matter what religion, sect, or cult it comes from. Take any tradition or belief from any religion, and if it's true, or even if it's just fun or fascinating or useful, it can be found in some form within Catholicism.

Let me give a few examples from the major religions. The strength of Islam is its passionate devotion to one God and to the teachings of the Book. In its case, the book is the Koran. Catholicism also passionately affirms the greatness of the one God and the truth of the Book (in its case, the Bible). Buddhism encourages a sublime transcendent spirituality with monks and celibacy and a life of contemplation. Ditto Catholicism. Judaism lives out a dynamic roller-coaster history of religion in which the people of God have tried to follow the law of God — sometimes with terrible, sometimes with glorious results. Same with Catholicism. Hindus enjoy a religion replete with statues, candles, ornate temples, colorful festivals, and terrible myths. Catholics do, too. New-Agers love chants, adore nature, burn incense, and meditate. So do Catholics. Shintoists venerate their ancestors with offerings of little rice cakes. Catholics offer Masses for theirs with little wafers of bread.

Do Anglicans have sublime literature, music, and architecture? Catholics also have a collection of pretty decent writers, composers, and cathedrals. Do Pentecostals speak in tongues and sing happy choruses? Plenty of Catholics do, too. Do the exclusive Brethren say that only members of their church may come to Communion? Catholics also preserve their holiest things for the initiates. Do Evangelical Christians love the Bible? Catholics established the Bible, and the best biblical scholars in the world are Catholic. Do the Amish eschew modern materialism to live an austere and holy communal life? So do Catholic monks and contemplative nuns.

These are but a few examples. They can be replicated time and time again. That is why when Catholics say, "I believe in the Communion of Saints," they're also saying, "I'm in union with all holy things."

The Catholic Church is essentially a church that says yes. If a thing is true, we Catholics will find a place for it. This is because a person is most often right in what he affirms and wrong in what he denies. When do most people begin to fall out with the Catholic

Church? When they begin to deny something that Catholics hold dear. So if you go into the Spanish cathedral and splutter, "But what are those chickens doing here? They're making a huge mess all over the floor!" good Catholics will tell you to stop being such a spoilsport. They're likely to say, "We forgot why those chickens are there, but we know they were there before you were. Let them be." They respond that way any time critics try to destroy something beautiful, good, true, or just plain fun within Catholicism. They come in and say, "You can't believe in a medieval superstition like transubstantiation!" or "You can't possibly have an infallible pope in this age of democracy!" And Catholics reply, "Oh, do leave it alone! It was here before you came along. You may not understand it, but destroying what you don't understand is the way of the boor and the vandal. Try to be civilized!"

Catholicism embraces everything good, and that really summarizes what a saintly person is as well. Perhaps the most famous saint of the modern age was a young French girl called Thérèse Martin, who summed it up when she said, "I will have all!" She wasn't being greedy; she was simply accepting everything in the universe as a good gift from God. For her that included misunderstanding, loneliness, and an excruciating death at an early age, but these things, too, she accepted as a gift.

When an ordinary person gets to the stage where even pain is understood as a special gift from Heaven, he is either mad or he has been changed into something greater than an ordinary person. The first Christians thought this was possible. They really did believe that Jesus Christ came not only to rescue the human race, but to transform it into his likeness. This means that individual human beings could actually become like Christ. The ramifications of this belief are astounding, for if Jesus Christ was God in the flesh, then these ordinary mortals came to realize that the long-term effect of becoming like Jesus Christ was that they were to become like gods themselves.

This is the other meaning of the phrase "Communion of Saints." It means that in this life we can be in constant contact with real human beings who have experienced this radical transformation. Furthermore, when we say we believe in the Communion of Saints, we mean we believe the saints in Heaven can actually do good on earth. On her terrible deathbed, Thérèse Martin had the audacity to claim, "I will spend my Heaven doing good on earth."[57] In other words, there is communication and commerce between earth and Heaven through these human beings who have been divinized.

Saying we believe in the Communion of Saints doesn't simply mean that we have ascribed to a certain intellectual proposition about saintly people. Belief in a statement means being alive to that statement and living within the very truth it testifies. Therefore, to believe in the Communion of Saints means we're in a constant fellowship with them. We're living in a relationship with the people who have been divinized — and if we're in their company, then we're one with them as we're one with members of our family. If we're kith and kin with the saints, then we're called to the same destiny, and this means we're called to pursue, in our own way, the same exhausting and exhilarating life they pursued. If this is true, then suddenly the whole Christian Faith becomes a lifelong journey of growth and change. Then the spiritual life is not just a matter of wandering up a gentle hill to enjoy the view. It's more like the ascent up a mountain. The way is steep and the weather sharp. We're all called to put on our boots and train hard for the climb. We're summoned to grapple with the ropes and pitons, negotiate the ledges, gasp in the thin air, and face the precipice, the narrow crumbling ledge, and the yawning abyss.

Once you've begun the ascent, you come to realize that this is what you're here for. You're here to be divinized, to be transformed into all that you were created to be. So you either decide to live in communion with the saints or not. You either climb the mountain or you don't climb the mountain. There's no room for half measures. So that same young girl who allowed this awesome and radiant transformation to take place in her life says to us, "You can't be half a saint. You must be a whole saint or no saint at all!"

We're right to be daunted. But this ascent is the only way to claim all things holy and infinitely precious for our own. Why are we surprised if they are hard to come by? Did we think that all things eternal in Heaven and earth would be ours for a bargain-basement price? These gifts might be free, but they're not cheap. While this may cause alarm, there is also cause for comfort, because the One who enabled the ascent in the first place is there as a guide. Furthermore, we don't climb alone, but with an army of family and friends; and at every moment, those who have gone before are just beyond us. They pause on the next ridge, their hearts filled with an inexpressible delight of love, and they call down, "Don't be afraid! There's more life to be lived, far more! We will give you a hand up! Come farther up and farther in!"

Chapter Seventeen

The Metanoia Mentality

. . . the forgiveness of sins . . .

Isn't it curious how confession is acceptable — and fashionable even — as part of self-help and group therapy, yet it's considered dark, neurotic, and guilt-ridden in the realm of religion? If you go to a therapist, you'll be encouraged to spill the beans because it's healthy. If you receive counseling, you'll be expected to haul all the skeletons out of your cupboard without shame. In an Alcoholics Anonymous group, the person next to you will be encouraged to say, "I'm George. I'm an alcoholic." But if you go to church and the person next to you shakes your hand and says, "I'm Mildred. I'm a sinner," you'll have your fears confirmed that the Church is full of fruit loops.

But Mildred shouldn't be blamed for being honest any more than George should. Surely one of the most obvious things any human being can say about himself is "I'm a sinner." Being a sinner simply means we haven't reached the glorious potential for which we were created. As the New Testament puts it, "All have sinned and fallen short of God's glory,"[58] and I remember an old Baptist preacher praying, "Dear Lord, forgive us for our falling shorts."

If we were created in God's image, then to have fallen short of God's glory means that we've missed being all that we should be. If we're destined for divinization, we've missed the target by a mile. This fact ought to be a constant nagging realization within our lives. And yet our instinct is to justify our failings and our laziness, and that, too, confirms the point that there's a kink in our nature.

Saying there's a kink in our nature isn't the same as saying we're evil through and through. Sometimes the way things appear is actually how they are, and simple observation tells me that I'm not all bad, and neither are most people. The idea that we're totally evil through and through is one of those pathological theological positions that has damaged millions of lives. We're created in God's image, so it's impossible for us to be evil at root. Even the worst, most vile human being still has a little shred of God's image within him. No, we're not totally depraved. But the image of God has been wounded or marred by our sinful inclinations. We need to be healed. The kink needs to be straightened out. The complex knot of our motives, desires, decisions, and actions needs to be untangled.

To say "I'm a sinner" isn't to grovel in the dust, wallowing in low self-esteem. It's simply to be honest about ourselves and admit that, while we have strengths, we also have weaknesses. Although we've learned a lot, we also have a lot to learn. Saying "I'm not all I could be" is a negative definition of sin. In other words, it's simply recognizing an absence. This is a good place to start, but very often falling short of our potential becomes the positive presence of all that we shouldn't be. When my laziness at 6:30 a.m. turns into irritability and I yell at the kids, my lack of potential becomes, not just something good undone, but something nasty done.

If our final destiny is to become all that we were created to be, and if we were created in God's image, then our ultimate destiny is to be divinized. But considering the evil of which we are capable, if it's possible to become radiant beings of goodness and light, it must also be possible to become snarling monsters of unspeakable evil and darkness. The troubling suspicion arises: if we're not headed in the direction of total transformation into God's image, we're most probably headed in the other direction. Despite our most fervent wishes, there's no cozy middle ground. Every journey ends up somewhere. It's better to decide on our destination while we're still on the journey than to discover in the end that we've caught the wrong bus.

Furthermore, to comprehend how totally nasty human beings can be, we only have to turn to the annals of crime and the horrors of history. Hitler's holocaust, the purges of Stalin, the killing fields of Cambodia and Rwanda, and the terrorist attacks of 9/11 illustrate the monstrous capability of man. The stories of serial killers, rapists, and child murderers remind each one of us of the other side of our potential.

Will we scale the heights of divinization or slide into the abyss of demonization?

Saying "I'm a sinner" is simply the first and most brutally honest admission that we've seen the way things are, and that we want to make the right choice. Our natural instinct, however, is to say that we're not sinners. Our first inclination is to defend ourselves, blame the other person, and justify what we've done. To say "I'm a sinner" requires a total shift in perception. There's a Greek word for this fundamental shift of awareness: *metanoia*, which means "turning around." In other words, to say "I'm a sinner" requires us to stand on our head.

When Christians go on to say they believe in "the forgiveness of sins," they're saying that once we make the first admission that we're sinners, and that we need something, there's help available.

There's a remedy for the sickness of sin. The knot can be untangled, and the twist can be put straight.

In this connection, Christians (and Catholics especially) are often blamed for spreading guilt. "Oh, the nuns were forever making us feel guilty!" is the weedy lament of the Catholic-school alum. But the nuns were there to teach children the truth, and it's an obvious truth that people are actually guilty. Did they want the nuns to lie? Their method of imparting this truth may not always have been kind or loving, but the truth still remains. Guilt is the natural, and useful, reaction to that truth: a kind of pain that naturally accompanies sin. It's a built-in reminder that sin is a sickness, and that any sickness that remains untreated may very well turn nasty and cause an awful lot of pain, heartache, and violence.

If you like, guilt is to sin what pain is to cancer. If you have cancer, you'll eventually have pain. If you sin, you'll suffer from guilt. If you have cancer, a good doctor doesn't say to you, "Oh, my dear! Are you suffering? I'll give you a pain killer, and then you'll feel better." On the contrary, the good doctor gathers his courage and says, "Let's talk straight. You're feeling pain because you have cancer, and the only remedy is going to be surgery followed by an awful dose of chemotherapy, and even then, you may not pull through." In a similar way, a good priest or nun doesn't say, "Are you feeling guilty, darling? Never mind. You're not really a sinner. You're just suffering low self-esteem. Just tell yourself you're a nice person, and you'll feel better." No, a good priest or nun says, "What are you feeling guilty about? Have you sinned? The remedy is to confess the sin, accept forgiveness, then go and make amends."

This process seems to me to be utter common sense. Any child who has fought on the playground knows that if he has done something wrong, he needs to say, "I'm sorry" and then put things right.

It's the same with any person's fault. Although the circumstances may be far more complicated, the principle is the same.

This brings us to forgiveness — one of those quirky ideas that Jesus Christ brought into the world. We take it for granted today that saying "I'm sorry" and forgiving people is the way to go. But it isn't so in other cultures. In fact, there are whole rafts of other ways for people to deal with things that have gone wrong. People might sacrifice virgins to appease the gods. They might pay a ransom to an injured party to put things right. They might cut themselves with knives, starve themselves, or dance in a whirling dervish to satisfy the angry gods. The most common recourse isn't forgiveness, but revenge; and to the ordinary mind, revenge makes sense. An eye for an eye and a tooth for a tooth seems to be a rather logical way of dealing with the problem.

Instead, Jesus Christ comes in with this absurd idea of forgiveness. Have you thought what this really means? It means that someone has the final power either to hold our sin against us or to lift the charge. Why should anyone have the nerve to claim such power? Where does it come from? This is precisely the question the religious leaders asked of Christ himself. When he forgave people, they said, "Who does this man think he is? Only God can forgive sins." They were correct, of course. Only God can forgive sins, because, as the Offended Party when sins are committed, he is the only one with that right. Moreover, only God can be the judge, and only God can be the judge because only God knows everything. Therefore only God can forgive sins and mete out just punishment. But when they accused Jesus Christ, what they didn't see was that in Jesus Christ, God was forgiving sin. In other words, when he claimed to forgive sins, Jesus Christ was making a huge claim. He was claiming that he himself had been given the authority on earth to do something that only God can do.

Adventures in Orthodoxy

This is the crunch point of the Christian Faith. Christianity is
first and foremost a religion of forgiveness. Forgiveness is the foundation on which the rest is built. The simple transaction is this:
Like George at the Alcoholics Anonymous meeting, human beings say, "I'm a sinner." Jesus Christ then says, "I forgive you, and
to prove that I have forgiven you, I will take the punishment for
your sin myself, and if you accept this astounding sacrifice, then
your slate will be wiped clean. You can get a fresh start, and then,
with your cooperation, we can solve your sin problem once and for
all. Furthermore, if you persevere, you will receive the power to
become like me. You can be an adopted son or daughter of God."

This transaction is not a "once and done" affair. It's a "once and
done over and over again" affair.

An old monk was asked what he did in the monastery all day.
His reply was "We fall and get up again. We fall and get up again."
If the Christian life is scaling a monumental mountain, then at
times we lose our step and fall down a crevasse. We get knocked off
the ledge and grab a tiny lip of rock by our fingertips. Sometimes
we stumble so badly that we plummet toward our deaths with only
the thin but unbreakable line of forgiveness to save us from our
fall. At times we climb the mountain in a driving snowstorm, unable to see the way. We may even climb on our hands and knees,
but still we climb. In fact, on this particular mountain, we may
come to realize that our very best progress is always made on our
knees.

Because of this you can immediately tell the authentic Christian from the phony. The phony thinks he has climbed the mountain already. The authentic Christian doubts whether he has
actually started yet. This is one of the tricks of the kingdom: the
ones who are furthest along really do believe they are at the back,
and the ones who think they are furthest up the mountain really

haven't left the training camp yet. In the Christian race, the last shall be first and the first last.[59]

That is why the Christian who is furthest along the journey repeats the simple prayer: "Lord Jesus Christ, Son of God, have mercy on me, a sinner." He has developed a *metanoia* mentality. He's constantly turning around; constantly checking his self-will and acknowledging that he's wrong. To one who doesn't understand, this constant prayer sounds like the depths of doom-and-gloom religion. Nothing could be further from the truth. Instead of being a paean of pessimism, it's a prayer of peace. For in that prayer, the simple soul repeats the essential human truth. In that prayer, he affirms the fundamental condition of the human race and declares with dignity, clarity, and joy what it means to be human: I need help. I cannot climb alone.

Chapter Eighteen

Cannibals, Crocodiles, and Corpses

. . . the resurrection of the body . . .

Schoolchildren who think about the resurrection of the body soon start asking delightfully gruesome questions. After all, if they've ever seen a cat hit by a car or gone to a funeral to see Uncle Mitch get lowered into the ground in a casket, they have a pretty good idea what happens. It doesn't take long to figure out that dead bodies decay and that Uncle Mitch, who sat them on his knee for a story and gave them huge bowls of ice cream, now lies very still in a box, going all gooey like the cat by the roadside.

Thus the difficulty of believing in the resurrection of the body. To put it bluntly, how can the body be resurrected if worms have eaten it and turned it into topsoil? The questions continue. What about Aunty Hazel, who loved doing crosswords and amateur dramatics? She was cremated, and her ashes can be seen in an urn on Uncle Bert's mantelpiece. Will those ashes be magically put back together again into an all-singing, all-dancing, puzzle-solving Aunty Hazel? Or what about people who were blown to bits by a bomb or were eaten by sharks or crocodiles, or lions and tigers and bears?

We don't want to insult God's accounting practices. We know he keeps track of every hair on our head and knows when every sparrow falls, but is he really going to keep track of every molecule of Uncle Mitch and Aunty Hazel and the missionaries who were eaten by cannibals? Will he track them all down and summon them all up to be put back together again like some vast cosmic jigsaw puzzle?

The question is a good one and ought to interest everyone, because we all have a curiosity about the gruesome details — otherwise we wouldn't slow down at traffic accidents. There are really only three ways around it. First, faced with the poetic foolishness of such an idea, we may simply opt for the atheist's solution and say there's no such thing as life after death. This would put us in a minuscule minority when faced with the huge number of human beings who do believe in life after death, but nevertheless, the atheist's solution, although it takes great faith and courage to adhere to, is one.

The second solution is that there's no such thing as the resurrection of the body, and instead we continue to exist in a merely spiritual state. But this is impossible to hold while still retaining any sense in which a particular person continues to exist as the same particular person. As soon as we start imagining Aunty Hazel existing on the other side, but without a body, she ceases to be Aunty Hazel and becomes an ectoplasm or an amoeba — just an amorphous something. We might try to imagine Aunty Hazel as just her personality or spirit, but as soon as we do, her smiling face appears, and we remember her belting out "There's No Business Like Show Business." In other words, Aunty Hazel can't exist as just pure personality because Aunty Hazel was always more than just a personality. She was a woman, with a woman's body expressing her personality.

Cannibals, Crocodiles, and Corpses

So if we believe in life after death, but not the resurrection of the body, we can't say a particular person continues to exist after death. That's why some religions say that in the afterlife we get rid of our bodies altogether and are simply absorbed back into the cosmic Spirit.

The third option is that we continue to exist as the people we are here and now, and to do that, we have to have bodies of some sort. We have to have bodies to be who we are, because, from day one, who we are has always included a body. Therefore, if we say we believe in life after death, then somehow or other, no matter how ridiculous it seems, we also have to believe in the resurrection body.

But maybe when we considered the problem of corpses that had turned to dust and ashes or been eaten by crocodiles and cannibals, we were taking the physical solidity of our bodies a bit too seriously. This is easy to do, because we're used to thinking of our bodies as this "too, too solid flesh." We imagine that this hairy, smelly, frustrating, and funny body that we love so much is a permanent fixture in the universe. We imagine that the body we occupy right here and now is the one we've always had. But it clearly isn't. Every seven years or so, all the cells of our body are renewed, so in a very real sense, the body I have now is a completely different body than the one I had seven years ago. By looking at old photographs, I can see that the body I have now has grown from that other one, but it's clearly a different body. Therefore, what we think of as a solid and permanent body is, in fact, quite a changeable thing. We're all shapeshifters. Our bodies are far more fluid and temporary than we think, and we mustn't be misled simply because the shapeshifting takes place over a relatively long period.

I make this point to introduce the idea that, although my physical body of cells and molecules totally changes every seven years or so, there is nevertheless another "body" that doesn't change. There is a physical part of me that is always me despite the changes. That photograph of me as a child doesn't picture the same body, but it does picture the same person. This brings us to the meaning of the word *body*.

In the Latin form of the Creed, we don't profess belief in the *corporis resurrectionem*, but in *carnis resurrectionem*. In other words, we profess belief specifically in the resurrection of the flesh. The theological definition of the word *flesh* comes from the Hebrews, who blessed the whole human race with a wonderfully sophisticated religious idea. They rejected the obvious idea that our bodies are shells or vehicles for our souls. Instead they thought that the flesh and the soul were permanently integrated and united. For them *flesh* meant much more than just the physical body. The whole person, with all the gifts of body, mind, and spirit, fused into one physico-spiritual being.

If this is so, then, rather than thinking of the soul as living in the body as a person lives in a house, perhaps we should think of the soul as dwelling in every cell of the body. Increasingly, biologists understand the mind in this way. So the mind doesn't seem to be limited only to the brain, but it's spread by the nervous system throughout the whole body. Likewise, the soul doesn't exist in one part of the body, but infuses the entire body, down to the tiniest cell and molecule. This is easy enough to suggest as a theory, but let us stand it on its head and say that if the soul dwells in every cell of the body, then maybe a bit of the body dwells in every part of the soul as well. After all, if we're a totally fused body-and-soul creation, this would follow. This suggests that, just as the mind and soul inhabit the body, so the body, in a sense, inhabits the mind and the soul. If that is so, there exists a kind of "soul body" that we could call the resurrection body. It has continuity with our mortal physical body, just as my lean boyhood body has continuity with the present fat and bald one. The soul body is derived from the earthly body, but it isn't subject to decay and change.

This shouldn't be so hard to imagine, because, as I've already pointed out, our bodies are changing all the time anyway. What if this "soul body," or resurrection body, simply blossoms at the point of death? After all, our physical bodies have gone through lots of changes throughout the course of our lives. This may simply be the final one. As a seed falls into the ground and dies in order to bring forth the flower, so our bodies fall into the ground and die to bring forth the resurrection body. And as the flower grows from the seed, but looks nothing like it, so it may be with our resurrection bodies. They're derived from these mortal bodies, but thrive and are alive with a new kind of life that has burgeoned forth from the old.

If the Resurrection of Jesus Christ is anything to go by, then this seems to be precisely what does happen. He rose from the dead, but people didn't recognize him at first. In a way, it was like seeing a boy at his college graduation whom you haven't seen for ten or twelve years. You scarcely recognize him, and yet you know the handsome, proud twenty-one-year-old is the same person as the gawky, buck-toothed nine-year-old with a snotty nose. So it will be in our own resurrection. We will have blossomed. We will have grown up to the full maturity of our years. We will be in our prime and will have reached that potential for which we were created.

Furthermore, there are hints that this bodily resurrection isn't just for us, but for the whole world. In a fascinating detail, St. Paul says the whole world "groans for redemption."[60] Like a woman giving birth, or like a person groaning in his final agony, the whole of creation is longing for this same resurrection. He seems to be hinting that the whole physical realm — every mountain and stone and tree, every flower and beast and fish and living thing — is also only partially made. Each one is surging forward to some as yet unrealized potential. Could it be that each and every living thing will also die and be recreated in a more perfect and fulfilled reality?

You and I and every living thing were created, only to be recreated through the transition called death. We are put here, along with the whole of creation, to become all that we were intended to be.

When we speak of the resurrection body, therefore, we speak of the soul-body person, totally united and completed. This resurrection body isn't something other than what we know now, but it's something transformed. Finally, as I have hinted elsewhere, this resurrection body isn't less physical than the present one, but more physical. It is to this poor, sad, broken-down body what a real person is to a black-and-white photograph of that person. The photo is monochrome, flat, and dead. The real resurrected person is in three-dimensional color. He lives and moves and laughs with uproarious joy. He is once and for all time, abundantly and everlastingly alive.

Chapter Nineteen

Eternity in a Grain of Sand

. . . and life everlasting.

Where would the science-fiction writers be without the fascinating "rubberiness" of time and space? How could they devise their stories without time machines, hyperspace, and teleportation? For that matter, where would the physicists and cosmologists be without the rich vein for speculation that space and time provide? Space and time are fascinating, because we can't avoid thinking about their limits, and as soon as we start to imagine their limits, we can't help but wonder if there are no limits. In other words, as soon as we think about space and time, we start to think about eternity.

For most people, eternity is awesome because it's big. Eternity is big because it goes on forever. But I've never really understood why we should feel awestruck when confronted by the vast expanses of time and space. In science we were taught about light years and parsecs and how planetary systems and galaxies were eons away, and it was all done in an atmosphere of hushed, awestruck whispers. But even if the distances were vast, I didn't understand why one ought to be amazed simply because something was big. Size doesn't equal value. A half-acre in Manhattan is worth more than ten thousand acres in Mississippi. Neither is size a sign of superiority. We don't consider an elephant more important than an infant.

I remember as a teenager suspecting that the awesomeness projected about the size of the universe was a diversionary illusion to take our minds away from the essential issue — like a little trick a magician uses to keep you from seeing the big trick he's about to pull off. The real issue was not quantity, but quality. The universe may be large, but it may also be empty. As a result, the life of one person on earth may be of more significance than entire galaxies. The main reason the vast distances of space seemed like an illusion to me was because they relied on the presumed stability of time. When you stop to think about it, we really experience distance, not as the measurement of cubits or kilometers or furlongs or feet, but as the amount of time it takes us to get from one place to another. It's more a measure of time than of space.

For us, then, if there were no such thing as time, there would be no such thing as distance. The vast cosmos, which we perceive with its endless array of galaxies and its limitless expanse of never-ending star systems, may not be vast at all. If time should be suspended, we would experience no distance between objects. If there were no time, wouldn't the universe shrink down to a very cozy size? If we could be everywhere at once, then we could also be in every time at once. Anything alive would exist in an everlasting single moment in which all events and all places existed in a suspended, yet dynamic unity.

There's a problem with this imaginative scenario. If everything exists in one timeless moment, it sounds dead and still. But if it's alive and active, it must move and change; and as soon as something changes or moves, it creates time, because there is then a sequence of events.

What if, however, that everlasting moment is somehow both at rest and in action at the same time? The one human activity where this seems to happen is in one of those courtly dances that we see in costume dramas from the eighteenth century. In such dances, everyone moves around and around in a set pattern, in a single action with one another and with the music. They're in constant harmonious motion and yet, in a way, they're at rest. Perhaps "life everlasting," or what we call Heaven, may be very like an eighteenth-century ball.

It may be, but I doubt that we'll all wear satin breeches and white powdered wigs. I doubt that the ladies in Heaven will have fans, feathers in their hair, and revealing décolletage. No. Instead, the figure of a ball, or a courtly dance, is an earthly image that serves well when we try to imagine how everlasting life can be active and in repose at the same time.

Most of all, life everlasting is characterized by the fact that we'll be outside of time. This sounds improbable to those of us who can only imagine life as something bound by time. But what if there really were such a thing as a timeless existence? When you contemplate the mystery of time, do you feel, as I do, that time is somehow provisional or temporary? Have you ever felt that by living in time you're living in an alien atmosphere? Do you ever suspect that you were made for another kind of existence — an existence unlimited by time?

Why else would you be so constantly confused and fascinated by time? If time were natural for us, why is it that when we think seriously about time, we almost always start to imagine what life would be like without it? When we think about oxygen, we don't start imagining what the world would be like without oxygen, because oxygen is as essential and natural to us as water is to a fish. But when we consider time, we always start to imagine timelessness.

Another thing that makes me suspect that time isn't our natural environment is that we're constantly surprised by the passage of time. You travel to visit your brother, and your niece comes into the room. You haven't seen her for two years, and you gasp, "Maggie! You've grown! I hardly recognized you!" Why should you be surprised by Maggie's growth unless you were surprised by time? Remember how quickly birthdays come around again, and how you can't imagine that you've really been married twenty-two years? Have you noticed how an hour was long when you were young and it grows shorter the older you become? What about that universal feeling that you're younger than you actually are: aren't you surprised at that old person who looks out of the mirror each morning? Why the constant amazement and amusement at time if we were made to be at home in time?

Similarly, haven't you felt most alive and most real in those precious and rare occasions when time seems suspended and you step outside your time-consciousness for a moment? This seems to happen in two ways, one mundane and one extraordinary. We often step outside our awareness of time when we are absorbed in some particular job or pastime that we enjoy. We are transported outside ourselves, and we suddenly glance at our watch and are amazed at how time has "flown by." Once again, this is everyday evidence that time isn't natural for us, and we're constantly surprised and irritated by both its fleetness and its length.

The other example is those extraordinary moments when we're taken outside time by some sudden experience of beauty, tragedy, truth, or joy. It may be as simple as a dust-filled shaft of sunlight on an autumn afternoon. It may be the laughter of a child, the tranquil beauty of a Chinese vase, the tears of an old widow, or a Raphael Madonna. It may be the hilarity of the circus, the thrill of a gripping story, or an exalted moment of love. In these moments of enlightenment, we're lifted beyond time into the timeless moment and so glimpse for a fleeting instant the very fringe of immortality.

When we say that we believe in life everlasting, we're affirming our suspicion that there's a timeless existence, and that this is the sort of existence we were made for. We were created to live in that timeless moment when our self-consciousness fades and we can be, not only real, but really integrated into our unique place in the intricate and simple dance of the whole creation. This life everlasting is the life of eternity, but it isn't meant to be enjoyed only in the afterlife.

Too often we imagine that this everlasting life is reserved for after death. We imagine that it's the reward. But the experience of children, poets, and saints tells us that this kind of life is actually available here and now. If everlasting life is one timeless moment, this moment right now is part of life everlasting. Standing on our head, we can ask whether there is any reality at all to time as it's popularly conceived. For the average person, does the past exist except in fond memories, feelings of regret, newspaper clippings, and archive film? Does the future exist except in imagination, anticipation, science fiction, and fear? Both past and future are ethereal and unreal to most of us, but this present moment is alive and real and, in a strange and fleeting way, just as eternal as the most everlasting life we can imagine. The fact that it's real makes it seem eternal, but the fact that it's fleeting reminds us that we're still trapped in time.

The saints are those people who have learned how to live each moment of life as if it were a little forever, and because they can do this, they live in a kind of heaven here and now. William Blake sang the same tune. He saw eternity in a grain of sand and said, "He who bends himself a joy/Does the winged life destroy/But he who kisses the joy as it flies/Lives in eternity's sunrise."[61] In other words, to live in that moment of perpetual flight and perpetual stillness is to live on the very edge of eternity here in this very moment. In contrast, to live in constant fear of the future or in anger and regret about the past is to make for ourselves a kind of living hell.

For those who master this eternal perspective, life is lived, like eternity, in a condition of dynamic repose. The courtly dance is one figure of this condition, but another is the joint symbol of the fire and the rose. Like the burning bush, everlasting life burns in a constant dynamic flame, constantly changing, yet never diminished. Along with everlasting fire, the mystical rose, complex and interleaved, stands as the sign of beauty and eternal calm repose. Together they are captured in the simple word *love*. Love is life everlasting. It's the force that moves the sun and the other stars, and yet remains constant and still.[62]

Here in this moment, and in the moment that is every moment, the saints are those who embrace both the fire and the rose. They live in "a condition of complete simplicity costing not less than everything" where the past has been reconciled and the future holds no fear. They do so because they have learned that "all shall be well and/All manner of thing shall be well/When the tongues of flame are in-folded/Into the crowned knot of fire/And the fire and the rose are one."[63]

Chapter Twenty

Let It Be

Amen.

One day, twenty years ago, in the Oriental section of the Victoria and Albert Museum, I discovered a pale-green Chinese vase. The small vase was ancient, beautiful, and frail. It stood with a few other pieces of china in a simple glass cabinet. I stopped for a moment and suddenly realized why someone would pay millions of dollars for such a treasure. I was captivated by its delicate and luminescent beauty. Somehow it cut across the barriers of time to bear the entire majesty of a Chinese dynasty, the mystery of a bygone age, and the exotic history of a foreign world. In its exquisite simplicity, it seemed to encapsulate the refined mind and manicured hands of its aristocratic owner, as well as the simple mind and soiled hands of the potter who made it. In that moment, I sensed a beauty, truth, and simplicity beyond words, so I quietly said the only word that applied: *Amen.*

Amen is simply a word of affirmation. It means "so be it" or "let it be." It means, "This is good and great beyond all my ideas and words, and I am struck into silence." It means, "This thing of beauty before me carries all things, and I stand before it as I stand beneath the sky at night, filled with mute wonder and humble gratitude at the simple magnificence of it all." This was my attitude before the ancient Chinese vase. This is my attitude before my beloved. This is also my attitude at the end of the Creed. At this point, the dogma takes me beyond dogma, and the words take me beyond words. This is the goal of worship: to take us beyond the blank words to tremble on the precipice of silence.

The Creed points us beyond the Creed, as the vase pointed beyond itself. Like the vase, the Creed is essentially a simple, every-day-useful thing. Its simplicity is in its practicality. Its eloquence is in its hard, practical language. The clue isn't to look too much at the Creed, but to look through it to contemplate the vast panorama of truth.

Those who dislike creeds point out that the particularity of creeds divides. But have you seen what causes the division? It's not the creed, but the denial of the creed. Those who say the Christian creed is divisive are like thieves who complain that laws against stealing infringe their personal freedoms. The Creed is simply an objective statement of beliefs. In itself it causes no division; indeed, it was designed to do exactly the reverse: to be a force for clarity and unity in a confused world.

If Christians were simply to affirm the Creed and not deny, arguments would never be necessary. In other words, if believers could only say a full and hearty *amen*, "let it be," we could all just let it be. The simple, monumental statements could stand, and the Creed would then be a focus for unity, not a source of division. This doesn't mean we never question, but that our questions are a passionate desire to know more of the mystery, not less. The Creed provides a starting point for further discovery. It's a ladder with which to climb, and all real inquiry should be taking us further up the ladder. A spirit of denial, on the other hand, forgets all that and constantly examines the ladder itself and questions whether it's strong enough, or whether it's a ladder at all.

The curious thing is that the very ones who seek to destroy the ladder go on to blame those who defend the ladder for being "divisive." Look at it this way: those who were climbing the ladder were taking it for granted and using it for its rightful purpose. Then, when they discovered someone lower down sawing away at the rungs, the climbers realized, not only that they might fall, but that the ladder wouldn't be intact for those who wished to follow. Then imagine their frustration when they come down to repair the ladder, only to find that they're being blamed for being argumentative, divisive, and obsessed with the ladder.

Unfortunately, all this theological fuss obscures the point of the Creed. The Creed isn't the whole story. It was never meant to be. It is merely a précis or a summary. The Creed isn't the final word; in fact, it's the *first* word. It's the first step on the journey, not the destination. The journey is conducted in a whole range of ways, of which theological reflection is only one part. Indeed, for most people, theological reflection scarcely comes into it. Instead, about the Creed they say, "Let it be," and the Creed becomes a kind of foundation on which the rest of their religious life is built. When integrated into a regular religious life, the Creed becomes a kind of support system.

So whether we're visiting the sick, campaigning for justice, worshiping at Church, praying or singing or studying, every religious action is upheld by the Creed, and through all these actions, we're living out the Creed. Furthermore, for the person of faith, the formal belief supports and enables his whole life. Whether he eats or drinks, or laughs or cries; whether he sleeps, works, thinks, or has a meal with friends, he's doing it all on the foundation of the Creed. Then as we live the Christian life, the words of that ancient formula work their way into our mind and heart and body. As they are acted out, the ideas transform the way we think.

If this transformation happens, the Creed has done its job. It has helped us, like the fat man, to stand on our head and see the world, ourselves, and all things from a fresh and true perspective. It has helped us to be real revolutionaries. The Creed can give us a wider perspective only because it first narrows down our perspective. It forces us to look at the subtle nuances of belief so that we can understand the wide panorama. The Creed helps us look at the specific in order to understand the general. It forces us to examine the details of diamonds so that we can see that each star is a diamond.

As the Chinese vase is a particular incarnation of universal beauty, so the Creed is a particular expression of universal truth. Like Jesus Christ himself, the Creed is scandalously particular. It's an intellectual embarrassment to imagine that the essential truths can be boiled down into such a short statement. But as Jesus Christ is the particular way into truth and life, so the Creed not only expresses the specific truths, but opens the door to the truth and life beyond expression.

The Creed, like the Chinese vase, is particular, but it's also practical. It works. It's beautiful, not only because it's simple and integrated, but because it points to an integrated beauty and truth beyond itself. The Creed provides a perspective. It gives us a mountaintop on which to stand, and from that summit we can breathe a clearer air and sometimes catch the strains of distant music. On that peak, there may be storms of confusion and fear, but if we wait, the clouds will clear, and there in a moment, a shaft of light will blaze down to reveal a glimpse of the endless sea.

This is where the Creed should bring us — not to theological dead ends, but to a world that never ends. Not to dull intellectual statements, but to the contemplation of Father, Son, and Holy Spirit. Not to a world that is closed and dying, but to a world that moves in ever-increasing spirals of glory, where the beautiful words are chanted time and again: as it was in the beginning, is now and ever shall be. World without end. World without end. World without end.

Amen.

Dwight Longenecker

Dwight Longenecker is an American who has lived in England for over twenty years. A former Anglican priest whose conversion to Catholicism appears in *Surprised by Truth 3*, he writes regularly for many magazines, papers, and journals in Britain, Ireland, and the USA.

Longenecker is the editor of a collection of British conversion stories called *The Path to Rome — Modern Journeys to the Catholic Faith* (Gracewing, 1999) and the author of *St. Benedict and St. Thérèse* (Gracewing/Our Sunday Visitor, Spring 2002) and *More Christianity* (Our Sunday Visitor, Autumn 2002).

At present Longenecker is writing a series of booklets called *Christianity Pure and Simple*. Commissioned by the Catholic Truth Society, they'll be used by Catholics in primary evangelization. Longenecker is also working on a play about the English Reformation and is about to finish his first novel.

As well as being a writer, he is an accomplished public speaker and broadcaster. He and his wife, Alison, have four children.

End Notes

Introduction

[1] G. K. Chesterton, *St. Francis of Assisi*.
[2] Christopher Taylor, *Socrates: A Very Short Introduction* (Oxford: Oxford Paperbacks, 2000).
[3] Richard Dawkins, *Unweaving the Rainbow* (London: Penguin, 1998).
[4] Tertullian. Cf. Henry Bettenson, trans. and ed., *The Early Christian Fathers* (Oxford: Oxford University Press, 1969).

Chapter One

[5] Friedrich Schleiermacher, *On Religion: Speeches to Its Cultured Despisers*, trans. R. Crouter (Cambridge: Cambridge University Press, 1988).
[6] Fyodor Dostoyevsky, *The Brothers Karamazov*.
[7] e. e. cummings, "yes is a pleasant country."

Chapter Two

[8] 1 Kings 19:11-13.
[9] Matt. 3:17.
[10] Cf. Mark 14:36.
[11] Martin Buber, *I and Thou*, trans. Ronald Smith (Edinburgh: T. and T. Clark, 1958).

Chapter Three

[12] Stephen Hawking, *The Universe in a Nutshell* (London: Bantam Press, 2001).

[13] *Fortean Times* is a "Journal of Strange Phenomena." Cf. Charles Fort, *Lo! New Lands, Wild Talents,* et al.

[14] G. K. Chesterton, *Orthodoxy.*

[15] St. Thomas Aquinas, *Summa Theologica.*

[16] C. S. Lewis, *The Magician's Nephew.*

[17] Cf. St. Augustine, *Confessions,* Bk. 10, ch. 27.

[18] Cf. Francis Thompson, "The Hound of Heaven."

Chapter Four

[19] William Blake, "Auguries of Innocence."

[20] From the *Star Wars* films.

[21] Matt. 18:3.

Chapter Five

[22] Matt. 10:34.

[23] Dylan Thomas, "The Force that Through the Green Fuse Drives the Flower."

[24] Gerard Manley Hopkins, "God's Grandeur."

[25] Gen. 32:24-29.

Chapter Six

[26] Cf. Luke 1:38.

[27] Luke 1:37.

[28] C. S. Lewis, *Mere Christianity.*

Chapter Seven

[29] John 18:38.

[30] Matt. 9:9; 12:30.

[31] Matt. 6:24.

[32] Cf. John 14:6.

[33] Cf. John 13:9.

Chapter Eight

[34] Isa. 53:3.
[35] John 19:30.
[36] Cf. Matt. 16:24.

Chapter Nine

[37] Related in Peter Stanford, *Heaven* (London: Harper Collins, 2001).
[38] Related in Leo Madigan. *What Happened at Fatima* (London: Catholic Truth Society, 2000).

Chapter Ten

[39] David Hume, *Dialogues Concerning Natural Religion and The Natural History of Religion* (Oxford: Oxford Paperbacks, 1998).
[40] Cf. John 10:10.
[41] Cf. 1 Cor. 15:14.

Chapter Eleven

[42] Cf. Acts 1:9.
[43] Cf. 1 Cor. 2:9.

Chapter Twelve

[44] Cf. Luke 11:20.
[45] Matt. 10:29, 30; 12:36.

Chapter Thirteen

[46] 1 Cor. 13:12.
[47] Cf. Luke 12:3.
[48] Cf. Ps. 36:9.
[49] Cf. Phil. 2:10-11.
[50] Cf. Matt. 6:26, 28.

Chapter Fourteen

[51] William Wordsworth, "Prelude."
[52] Percy Shelley, "Hymn to Intellectual Beauty."

[53] William Wordsworth, "Lines Above Tintern Abbey."
[54] Cf. Rom. 8:15, 23; Gal. 4:5; Eph. 1:5.

Chapter Fifteen

[55] Luke 6:26.
[56] Matt. 16:18.

Chapter Sixteen

[57] St. Thérèse of Lisieux, *Story of a Soul.*

Chapter Seventeen

[58] Cf. Rom. 3:23.
[59] Cf. Matt. 19:30.

Chapter Eighteen

[60] Cf. Rom. 8:22.

Chapter Nineteen

[61] William Blake, "Eternity."
[62] Dante, *The Divine Comedy*, "Paradise."
[63] T. S. Eliot, "The Four Quartets."

Sophia Institute Press®

Sophia Institute® is a nonprofit institution that seeks to restore man's knowledge of eternal truth, including man's knowledge of his own nature, his relation to other persons, and his relation to God. Sophia Institute Press® serves this end in numerous ways: it publishes translations of foreign works to make them accessible to English-speaking readers; it brings out-of-print books back into print; and it publishes important new books that fulfill the ideals of Sophia Institute®. These books afford readers a rich source of the enduring wisdom of mankind. Sophia Institute Press® makes these high-quality books available to the public by using advanced technology and by soliciting donations to subsidize its publishing costs. Your generosity can help Sophia Institute Press® to provide the public with editions of works containing the enduring wisdom of the ages. Please send your tax-deductible contribution to the address below.

For your free catalog, call:
Toll-free: 1-800-888-9344

Sophia Institute Press® ◆ Box 5284 ◆ Manchester, NH 03108
www.sophiainstitute.com

Sophia Institute® is a tax-exempt institution as defined by the Internal Revenue Code, Section 501(c)(3). Tax I.D. 22-2548708.